How to Parent Boys With ADHD

Simple Strategies to Build Focus, Strengthen Self-Regulation, and Help Him Thrive at School and at Home

Adam Tian

This book is not a substitute for professional counseling or therapy.

Every child with ADHD is different, and the strategies presented in this book may not be appropriate for all situations. If your son is experiencing severe behavioral difficulties, significant academic challenges, emotional distress, or if you have concerns about his mental or physical well-being, please consult a licensed pediatrician, child psychologist, or ADHD specialist. In cases of crisis or emergency, contact your local emergency services immediately.

This guide is designed to provide practical, evidence-based strategies for parents of boys with ADHD. It draws on established frameworks in behavioral psychology, positive parenting, and neurodevelopmental research. The tools and techniques presented here can be used independently or as a structured companion to professional support. Individual results vary depending on each child's unique profile, environment, and consistency of practice.

If you are currently working with a therapist, counselor, or pediatric specialist, consider sharing this book with them. It can serve as a valuable resource between appointments. If you are navigating this journey independently and find that your son's challenges are not improving after several months of consistent effort, or if they worsen, seeking professional guidance is strongly recommended.

Table of Contents

About Me and Why I Wrote This Book

I still remember the exact moment I realized I had no idea what I was doing.

It was a Tuesday evening. My son, Marcus, was nine years old. He'd come home from school with a crumpled note from his teacher stuffed in the bottom of his backpack -- one of those notes you almost miss because they're folded so many times they look like a piece of garbage. I read it standing in the kitchen while he was already in the other room, making what I can only describe as the sound of a small tornado.

The note said, in careful, polite teacher language, that Marcus was "struggling to stay on task" and "having difficulty managing his impulses during group work." It was the third note that month. I put it on the counter next to the others.

Then I walked into the living room, looked at my son -- who had somehow pulled every single cushion off the couch and was jumping between them like they were stepping stones -- and I said, with a calm I absolutely did not feel: "Marcus. Stop."

He looked at me. He kept jumping.

And I just stood there, not knowing what to do next.

That was the start of a long few years.

Marcus was diagnosed with ADHD when he was eight. By the time that Tuesday happened, we'd already been through the initial appointments, the evaluations, the conversations with specialists who handed us pamphlets and told us to "stay consistent." We had the diagnosis. We had the information. What we didn't have was any real sense of how to live with it, day after day, in a house that felt like it was always one bad afternoon away from falling apart.

I'm not a psychologist or a therapist. I'm a dad who coaches youth soccer on weekends, who makes pasta with too much garlic because I find cooking relaxing, and who spent a long time thinking that if I just tried harder, read one more book, found the right system, everything would click into place.

It didn't work like that.

What I found in most parenting books on ADHD was information. A lot of it. Brain science, behavior charts, reward systems. Some of it was genuinely useful. But none of it felt like it was talking to me -- a person who was exhausted, who sometimes lost his temper and felt guilty about it for days, who didn't need a lecture on neurodevelopment at ten o'clock at night. I needed someone to tell me the real stuff: what to do when nothing works. How to talk to your son when he's flooded and not listening. How to stop taking it personally. How to keep going.

I started writing notes for myself. Not for a book -- just to make sense of what was working and what wasn't. Conversations with other parents of kids with ADHD, most of which happened in parking lots after soccer practice or in hushed tones at school pickup. Research I read during my lunch breaks at work, some of which changed how I saw my son completely. Small adjustments we made at home that turned out to matter more than any formal system we'd tried.

Slowly, something started to shift. Not in Marcus -- he was still Marcus, full speed, all the time. But in how I showed up for him. In what I expected. In the moments when I was able to hold steady instead of reacting. And in the relationship between us, which had been strained in ways I hadn't fully admitted to myself.

I wrote this book because I wish someone had handed it to me three years ago. Not a textbook. Not a collection of clinical advice dressed up in warm language. Something honest, practical, and written by someone who had actually lived in the middle of it.

If any of this sounds familiar -- the notes from teachers, the evenings that go sideways, the feeling that you're doing everything you can and it's still not enough -- then this book is for you. I'm not here to tell you I figured it all out. I'm here to share what I learned, what helped, and what I would have done differently. That's all this is.

You're not failing. You're figuring it out. Let's do that together.

Introduction

You already know what ADHD is.

You have read the pamphlets. Sat through the appointments. Watched the videos, bookmarked the articles, listened to other parents describe what worked for them. You have tried the reward charts and the timers and the routines and the firm consequences and the gentle ones. Some of it helped. Some of it made things worse. Most of it worked for a few weeks and then stopped working for no clear reason, which is its own kind of exhausting.

And yet here you are.

That gap, the one between understanding what your son has and figuring out how to actually live with it every single day, is exactly what this book is about. Not the diagnosis. Not the neuroscience in its full technical form. Not the theory. The daily reality: the mornings that go sideways before anyone has finished breakfast, the homework sessions that turn into something neither of you wanted, the moments when you say the exact wrong thing and watch your son shut down, and you replay it for hours afterward wondering what you should have done instead.

Parenting a boy with ADHD is invisible work in a way that other kinds of caregiving are not. There is no external marker that tells the world this child is working harder than he looks. What people see is a boy who interrupts, who loses things, who argues about everything, who seems not to listen even when you know he heard you. What they do not see is the effort it takes him to hold himself together at school for six hours and then fall apart the moment he walks through your door. They do not see the frustration he feels when his own brain will not cooperate. They do not see how much he wants to do better, and how much it costs him when he cannot.

You see it. That is why you are reading this.

This book is not a promise that things will become easy. Boys with ADHD are not problems to be fixed. They are kids with specific brains, specific needs, and, if you look at the right things in the right light, specific strengths. Raising them well is less about finding the perfect system and more about understanding how their brains actually work, then building your responses from that understanding outward.

What you will find in these pages is direct, practical guidance on the parts of this journey that most books skip. What to do when your son is flooded with emotion and nothing you say is landing. How to talk to teachers who interpret his behavior as attitude when it is not. How to discipline in a way that actually teaches something instead of just creating more conflict. How to protect your relationship with him during the years when that relationship is under the most strain.

Each chapter covers one piece of the larger picture. You can read them in order, or you can go straight to the chapter that covers what you are dealing with right now. The book is organized to support both approaches. Some chapters will feel immediately relevant. Others will become more relevant as your son gets older, or as the challenges shift, because they do shift.

You are not too late, no matter where you are starting from. The research on this is consistent: children with ADHD who have at least one parent who genuinely understands how their brain works, and who keeps showing up even when it is hard, do significantly better over time. Not perfectly. Not without struggle. But better, in ways that compound over years.

That parent can be you.

Let's get started.

Chapter 1: What ADHD Actually Looks Like in Boys

The brain that is wired differently is not broken. It is running a different operating system.

Picture two boys sitting in the same third-grade classroom on the same Tuesday afternoon. Same teacher, same assignment, same amount of time. The first boy puts his head down and works. Twenty minutes later, his worksheet is done and he is looking out the window. The second boy has written his name, put down his pencil, picked it back up, sharpened it twice, looked around the room several times, written two words, erased one of them, and is now whispering something to the kid beside him.

By the end of the school year, the first boy's teacher will describe him as focused and hardworking. The second boy's file will include words like distractible, impulsive, and not working to his potential. Both descriptions are accurate. What neither one explains is why the second boy functions the way he does, or what that means for how to actually help him.

Understanding ADHD in boys starts here: not with a list of symptoms, but with a clearer picture of what those symptoms look like in practice, where they come from, and why the standard responses to them so often fall short.

Why Boys With ADHD Get Misunderstood More Often

ADHD shows up differently depending on who has it, and in boys the presentation tends to be louder. More physical. More visible. A boy who cannot sit still, who blurts things out during a lesson, who gets up from his chair when everyone else is seated, who starts a fight on the playground over a rule nobody else cared about, is hard to miss. What is easy to miss is the reason behind all of it.

Boys are diagnosed with ADHD at roughly twice the rate of girls, and their symptoms are more likely to be externalized: running, climbing, shouting, grabbing, pushing. The kind of behavior that gets a referral to the office and eventually to an evaluation. The problem is that "external" and "behavioral" are not the same thing, even though they get treated as if they are. External behavior in a child with ADHD is not a choice. It is the output of a brain that is managing input differently, in a body that is trying to regulate itself through movement and stimulation because sitting still feels genuinely unbearable.

When a boy drums his fingers on a desk, it is not to annoy his teacher. When he interrupts a conversation, it is rarely to be rude. The impulse arrives before the consideration of consequences, and the gap between those two things is where most of the misunderstanding lives. Teachers see the behavior. They do not see the brain. And the behavior, at face value, looks a lot like deliberate choices: choosing not to pay attention, choosing to disrupt the class, choosing not to finish the assignment. This framing leads to responses that make perfect sense if the child is making choices, but have very little effect on a child who is not. More reminders. More consequences. More conversations about respect and responsibility. The child hears them, agrees to do better, and then does the same thing again next week. Adults interpret this as defiance. It is not defiance. It is a brain struggling to do something it has not yet learned to do consistently.

The history of ADHD research adds another layer to this. Early studies on the disorder were conducted almost entirely on boys, which is one reason the hyperactive presentation became the default image. Girls with ADHD, who more often present with inattention rather than hyperactivity, spent years being overlooked because they did not match that template. But even within the male presentation, there is far more variation than the stereotype suggests. Not every boy with ADHD is running around the classroom. Some sit very still and stare at nothing. Some are charming and funny and make friends easily but cannot track a single assignment for more than a few hours. Some perform well in one-on-one settings and fall apart the moment a group is involved. The diagnosis covers a range, not a type, and boys who fall outside the loud, physical end of that range are still regularly missed or explained away.

That phrase "just being a boy" shows up often in the stories parents tell about the years before a diagnosis. Teachers who said he would settle down eventually. Relatives who pointed to their own childhood as evidence that all boys were like this. Pediatricians who suggested waiting another year. Sometimes that waiting stretched into several years. During that time, a child was being held to a standard his brain was not yet equipped to meet, without anyone identifying the actual reason why.

The cost of that misattribution is real. A boy who is told repeatedly, directly or by implication, that he is not trying hard enough begins to build a story about himself from that evidence. The academic record fills up with "not working to his potential." The behavioral record fills with incidents. The child draws conclusions. Getting the picture right is not just about accuracy. It is about interrupting that story before it calcifies into identity.

The 3 Types of ADHD and What They Mean for Your Son

Many parents leave their son's diagnostic appointment with a label and not much else. The term covers significant ground, and what ADHD looks like in one child can be strikingly different from what it looks like in another. That difference matters, because understanding your son's specific presentation changes what you look for, what you work on, and what kind of support is most likely to land.

The diagnostic framework currently recognizes three presentations. The first is predominantly inattentive. A child in this category has difficulty sustaining focus, misses details, loses things regularly, and appears to be listening when he is not quite there. He is not hyperactive in the physical sense. He does not run or climb or interrupt. He sits quietly and stares at the wall, or reads the first paragraph of an assignment several times without absorbing it, or starts something with genuine interest and drifts away before it reaches the halfway point. In a classroom this child often goes unnoticed for years. He is not causing problems. He is just not quite present, and absence is easier to overlook than disruption.

The second presentation is predominantly hyperactive-impulsive. This is the one most people picture when they hear ADHD. The child who cannot sit still, who talks constantly, who acts before thinking, who grabs things without asking and interrupts conversations mid-sentence and struggles in any situation that requires sustained waiting. At school this presentation tends to be identified early, because it is hard to overlook. At home it can make ordinary situations feel like negotiations with someone who has no off switch.

The third presentation, combined type, involves meaningful symptoms in both areas. Inattentive on some tasks, hyperactive-impulsive in others, or both at once depending on the setting. This is the most common presentation in boys who receive a diagnosis.

What matters practically is not just which category your son has been labeled with, but which situations reliably bring out which symptoms. A boy with combined type might sit absorbed through a long movie and be completely unable to read a page of a textbook for five minutes. The capacity for sustained attention is clearly present; the question is what activates it and what shuts it down. That inconsistency is one of the most disorienting things about ADHD for parents and teachers alike. It feeds the reading of laziness, of selective attention, of choosing when to try. He is not being selective. His brain is responding to interest and stimulation in a way that most people's brains do not.

One thing worth knowing about presentations: they shift. A boy who is primarily hyperactive at age seven may look more inattentive at age twelve. This is not because the ADHD has improved or faded. It is because hyperactivity tends to decrease as children grow and develop better physical regulation, while inattentive symptoms, which were always there but easier to mask, persist and become more visible as academic demands increase. Parents who were told their son was "so much better now" in middle school sometimes find themselves blindsided when high school arrives. The underlying wiring has not changed. The difficulty of the environment has.

Knowing your son's specific presentation helps you stop asking "why can't he just" and start asking "given how his brain works, what would actually help here." That shift in framing is where most of the useful work begins.

One other thing the type categories do not capture: intensity. Two boys can both have combined-type ADHD and live completely different daily experiences depending on how severe their symptoms are and how well their environment accommodates them. The diagnosis opens a door; it does not tell you everything about what is on the other side. That part comes from observation, from paying close attention to your specific son over time, noticing what settings calm him and what settings wind him up, what topics pull him in and what tasks reliably fall apart, what time of day he is most available and what conditions make him unavailable entirely. The label gives you a map. Your son gives you the territory.

What the Research Really Says About the Male ADHD Brain

There is a version of the ADHD brain explanation that gets passed around in pamphlets and parent-night presentations, the one where someone draws a dopamine molecule and talks about chemical imbalances. It is not wrong, exactly, but it does not give parents much to work with. A more useful frame is one that connects the neuroscience to what you actually see at the kitchen table.

The brain's prefrontal cortex is responsible for a set of capacities that researchers group under the term executive function: the ability to plan ahead, start tasks, organize information, regulate impulses, manage time, and monitor your own behavior as you go. In children with ADHD, this region of the brain develops more slowly than in neurotypical peers, and it functions differently even once it matures. The gap between an ADHD child and a same-age peer in terms of prefrontal development is estimated at roughly three years in early childhood, shrinking somewhat over time but never fully closing for many people.

This is not a minor gap. It means that a ten-year-old with ADHD may have the executive function of a seven-year-old in terms of how reliably he can initiate tasks, regulate his frustration, or remember the steps of a multi-part instruction. It does not mean his intelligence is lower. IQ and executive function are separate systems. Some of the sharpest, most creative minds in any room are running on a prefrontal cortex that is genuinely less consistent at the kinds of self-management that school and daily life require.

The dopamine piece matters too, but not in the way it is often explained. In an ADHD brain, the regulation of dopamine in certain circuits is less efficient. Dopamine is the neurotransmitter most closely associated with motivation, reward anticipation, and the sense that an activity is worth pursuing. When dopamine signaling is unreliable, the brain has trouble generating that "this is worth doing" signal for tasks that are not immediately interesting or rewarding. This is why your son can spend three hours on something that captivates him and cannot spend ten minutes on something that does not, regardless of how important you tell him the second thing is. The importance does not create dopamine. Interest does, novelty does, urgency does, challenge does. School assignments, on a typical afternoon, often generate none of the above.

Russell Barkley, one of the most cited researchers on ADHD, describes it not as a disorder of attention but as a disorder of self-regulation: the capacity to manage your own behavior across time in service of future goals. That definition reframes a lot of what parents observe. The child who cannot stop himself from grabbing something. The child who starts projects and abandons them. The child who knows the test is tomorrow and still does not study. These are not failures of character or effort. They are failures of a regulatory system that is still catching up with the demands being placed on it.

What this means for you, practically, is that external structure compensates for internal structure that is not yet online. The child cannot create his own regulation reliably, so you provide it through routines, reminders, environment design, and scaffolding, not as indulgence but as a bridge to the capacities that are developing, just on a slower schedule.

It also means that inconsistency is not hypocrisy. A boy who completes a complex Lego set over four hours and cannot write two sentences of a book report is not being manipulative. The Lego set generated enough novelty and immediate feedback to sustain his engagement. The book report did not. Both things are true simultaneously. Parents who understand this stop spending energy arguing about fairness and start spending it on designing conditions where the brain can actually engage. That is a much more productive place to put the work.

How ADHD Presents Differently Across Age Groups

ADHD does not stay the same as a child grows. The behaviors change. The challenges change. What worked at one stage stops working at the next. Parents who understood their son's ADHD at age eight often feel like they are starting over when he turns thirteen, because in important ways they are. The condition is the same; the version of it they are living with has changed.

In the preschool years, ADHD tends to look like intensity without brakes. The child is everywhere at once, cannot tolerate being stopped or redirected, has meltdowns that are bigger and longer than other children his age, and needs constant engagement to stay regulated. At this stage it is hard to distinguish ADHD from typical development at the extreme end of the normal range, which is part of why early diagnosis is complicated and controversial. That said, children who will later be diagnosed often look noticeably different from their peers even at three and four, not just "active" but in a different category of difficulty.

In the elementary school years, the academic structure of school begins to put real pressure on the executive function deficits. Reading comprehension, multi-step math, written assignments, sitting at a desk for extended periods: all of these demand the precise capacities that ADHD compromises. This is when many children first receive a diagnosis, often triggered by a teacher raising concerns. Socially, boys with ADHD may start having friction with peers at this stage: they play too rough, they do not read the group's cues, they say the thing everyone was thinking but nobody was going to say. Their intensity can be fun and then, suddenly, too much.

Middle school often brings a sharp increase in difficulty, for reasons that are structural. The child now has multiple teachers instead of one, each with different expectations and communication styles. He is responsible for tracking assignments across subjects without a single adult who sees the full picture. The social stakes are higher, and the tolerance for social awkwardness is lower. Many boys with ADHD who were managing adequately in elementary school hit a wall in sixth or seventh grade. This is not a regression. It is a mismatch between the new demands and a regulatory system that has not kept pace.

In high school, the picture often becomes more complex because adolescence adds its own layer. Hormonal changes can amplify both impulsivity and emotional reactivity. The academic workload increases. The social landscape expands. Some boys develop coping strategies that help them manage; others start avoiding, or finding ways to mask the difficulty through behavior that looks like attitude or indifference. A teenager who suddenly seems not to care may be a teenager who has run out of ways to cope with caring too much.

The practical value of understanding these stages is that it helps you stay calibrated. The strategies you need when your son is eight are not the strategies you will need when he is fifteen. And the challenges that feel overwhelming at one stage often ease at the next, while new ones take their place. The work is ongoing, but it is not the same work throughout.

One thing that does not change across the stages: your son's need for at least one adult in his life who sees his behavior accurately. Not as defiance or laziness or attitude, but as the output of a brain at a particular point in its development, under a particular amount of pressure. That adult does not have to be perfect. They just have to keep looking clearly, even when the picture is difficult to see.

The Common Myths That Make Everything Harder

ADHD carries more misinformation per square inch than almost any diagnosis in common circulation. Some of that misinformation comes from outdated research. Some of it comes from cultural skepticism toward the diagnosis itself. Some of it comes from well-meaning people who are working from incomplete information. Whatever the source, the myths do real damage, and the first step to getting past them is naming them directly.

The most persistent myth is that ADHD is not a real condition, that it is a label invented to explain away normal childhood behavior, a product of impatient parents and overzealous pharmaceutical companies. The research does not support this. ADHD has been studied for more than a century, appears across cultures and socioeconomic groups, shows consistent neurological differences on brain imaging, has a significant genetic component, and responds to specific interventions in predictable ways. Disagreement about how often it is diagnosed, or whether it is sometimes over-diagnosed, is a legitimate conversation. The existence of the condition is not.

A second myth is that boys outgrow ADHD. Some symptoms do decrease as children develop, particularly the hyperactive-impulsive ones. But the underlying differences in brain wiring do not disappear. Roughly 60 to 70 percent of children with ADHD continue to meet diagnostic criteria as adults. Many adults who no longer meet the full criteria still experience meaningful impairment from subclinical symptoms. "He'll grow out of it" is, at best, an incomplete story.

The medication myths deserve their own entry. The idea that ADHD medication turns children into zombies, or changes their personality, or is a form of chemical restraint, gets repeated enough that many parents enter the medication conversation already afraid. The reality is more nuanced. Stimulant medication is the most studied treatment for any childhood psychiatric condition, and for children who respond to it, the effect is typically an increase in the child's ability to access who they already are, not a flattening of their personality. Side effects are real and need to be monitored. Medication is also not a complete solution on its own. But the fear of medication keeping families from an effective tool, while a child struggles daily, is worth examining honestly.

There is also the idea that ADHD comes from bad parenting, too much screen time, sugar, or food dyes. Diet and screens can affect behavior in children generally, with or without ADHD, and good structure genuinely helps ADHD brains. None of these things cause the disorder. ADHD is largely genetic, with heritability estimates in twin studies ranging from 70 to 80 percent, comparable to the heritability of height. Parents did not create this by being inconsistent or permissive, and they will not fix it by getting stricter.

The last myth on this list is the one that does the most damage in the long run: the idea that ADHD means a child is not smart. Many boys with ADHD are highly intelligent. Some are exceptionally so. Intelligence and executive function are distinct systems, and high intelligence does not protect against ADHD, nor does ADHD reduce intelligence. What it creates is a gap between what a child is capable of and what he can consistently produce under standard conditions. That gap is not a measure of his mind. It is a measure of the mismatch between how his brain works and how most classrooms are structured.

Clearing these myths is not a minor task. They are the background noise against which every conversation about your son takes place, inside your own head and with the people around you. The clearer you are on what is actually true, the less energy you spend defending something that does not need defending, and the more you have for the work that actually matters.

Chapter 2:
Inside Your Son's Head

ADHD is not a problem of knowing what to do. It is a problem of doing what you know.

Your son sits down at the kitchen table, homework in front of him. You ask if he knows what he needs to do. He tells you, clearly and in the correct order: read the chapter, answer the five questions, check his work. You walk away. Eight minutes later you come back and he is building something out of rubber bands and staring at the ceiling. You ask what happened. He has no answer, and the look on his face tells you he genuinely does not know.

This is not a performance. It is not stubbornness dressed up as confusion. Something real happened in those eight minutes, something that most explanations of ADHD skip because it takes place inside a system most parents never get a clear picture of. Getting that picture changes everything about how you interpret your son's behavior, because once you can see what is actually driving the moments that currently look like attitude, laziness, or deliberate sabotage, those moments stop being about character and start being about a brain doing its best with what it has.

This chapter is about the inside view. The functional systems that shape how your son experiences every hour of every day, and why those systems produce the behaviors you are trying to understand.

Executive Function and Why Your Son Cannot Just Try Harder

The phrase "executive function" appears constantly in conversations about ADHD and rarely gets explained in a way that is actually useful to someone living with the daily consequences. Executive function is not one capacity. It is a cluster of mental systems that work together: the ability to start a task without needing to be told twice, to hold a plan in mind while executing it, to shift from one activity to another when the situation changes, to monitor your own progress without external checkpoints, and to manage the emotional resistance that arises when the task is boring, difficult, or unrewarding. Together these systems act as the brain's management layer. Not the worker doing the job, but the coordinator who decides what job to do, in what order, with what resources, and how to adjust when something is not going to plan.

In most people, this management layer runs quietly in the background. The reminder to do something arises, the person acts on it, and the transition happens with almost no conscious effort. The override of procrastination, the shift from one task to the next, the monitoring of time while working toward a deadline: all of these happen without requiring the person to consciously engage the system. For a child with ADHD, that background firing is inconsistent. Not absent, but unreliable in a way that changes completely based on the nature of the task.

This inconsistency is the detail that confuses parents most, and the detail that most consistently gets misread as selective effort. You have watched your son sit with complete absorption for two hours working on something he chose, without any reminder, without any reward, without any management from you at all. You have also watched him leave a five-minute task undone for three days despite daily reminders, full knowledge of the consequence, and repeated conversations in which he agreed to do it. The obvious interpretation of that gap is that he is choosing when to try. The accurate interpretation is that two completely different brain activation pathways are involved, and only one of them is firing.

Physician William Dodson's concept of an interest-based nervous system explains the mechanism. Where most people's brains activate on importance and logical priority, the ADHD brain activates primarily on interest, challenge, urgency, and novelty. These are not choices or preferences. They are the triggers that actually open the gate between wanting to do something and the management system coming online to execute it. When the activity generates enough of those triggers, the management system activates and the child can work as well as or better than anyone. When the activity does not generate those triggers, the management system does not respond to reasoning, deadlines, promises of reward, or appeals to future consequences. The gate stays closed, not because the child is refusing to open it, but because the input required to open it is not present.

This means that telling your son to just try harder is not a useful instruction, not because it is unsympathetic, but because it misidentifies the problem. Effort is not what is missing. Access is what is missing. The gate between knowing what to do and doing it is not opening, and more effort does not open a gate that is controlled by a different mechanism entirely. Understanding this does not mean removing expectations. It means redirecting the question from "why won't he" to "what conditions make it possible for him to," and that question has actual answers.

What it looks like on an ordinary Tuesday is a child who cannot start his English assignment for forty minutes, then sits down to do it for a reason that makes no logical sense from the outside (the teacher mentioned a consequence, or he overheard you on the phone, or his brother walked by and said something that created just enough urgency) and finishes it in twenty minutes. You want to know why it could not happen forty minutes ago. The answer is that forty minutes ago the gate was closed. The urgency input had not arrived yet. Now it has.

The Emotional Dysregulation Nobody Warned You About

Parents are typically told at diagnosis that their son may be hyperactive, inattentive, and impulsive. Almost no one is told that he may also experience emotions that hit harder, faster, and last longer than the same emotions do in other children. This omission is significant because for many families, the emotional piece is where the hardest daily difficulties live.

Children with ADHD feel emotions at a higher intensity than neurotypical peers and return to baseline more slowly after an emotional peak. The surge arrives faster than expected, reaches a higher point than the situation seems to warrant, and the period of coming back down is longer. This is not because the child is oversensitive or immature in a general way. It is because the same regulatory system that handles task initiation and impulse control also handles emotional regulation, and in the ADHD brain that system runs the same inconsistent way across both domains. The child who cannot reliably stop himself from grabbing something is often also the child who cannot reliably stop an emotion before it becomes an outburst.

In boys, this pattern frequently presents as anger rather than sadness or anxiety, which is why it so often gets interpreted as attitude or aggression. A correction that registers as mild to most children registers as a significant hit to a child with emotional dysregulation. A disappointment that another child would process and move past in a few minutes can anchor in an ADHD child for hours. The parent who thought the incident was over at lunch finds out at dinner that it was not, because the child is still carrying it.

One specific pattern within this deserves its own name. Rejection Sensitive Dysphoria describes an intense emotional response to the perception of being criticized, left out, or having failed in someone's eyes. The word perception is important. The trigger does not have to be real rejection or real criticism. A parent using a neutral tone on a difficult morning can register as disappointment. A teacher marking an answer wrong in front of the class can register as public humiliation. A friend who does not respond to a text can register as being ignored. The emotional response to these perceived events is not calibrated to what actually happened. It is calibrated to how the nervous system processed what happened, which in an ADHD brain is processing it through a much more sensitive filter.

In boys, Rejection Sensitive Dysphoria frequently comes out as explosive anger or complete shutdown. The child who appeared fine ten seconds ago suddenly goes from zero to furious, or closes down entirely and refuses to engage. Parents who do not know about this pattern often spend enormous energy trying to talk the child through it rationally, explaining that no one was actually criticizing him, asking him to calm down and be reasonable. This does not work during an episode because the emotional flood has temporarily disrupted access to the reasoning centers that would need to process those inputs. The rational conversation can happen after, never during.

What you can do during an episode is create the conditions for the flood to recede: physical space, a calm presence, no new demands, and no attempts to argue or explain. This feels counterintuitive because the behavior looks like defiance and instinct says address it now. Addressing it now makes it longer and louder. Letting the flood pass and addressing it afterward makes it shorter and creates an actual opening for learning. This is one of the most counterintuitive things about parenting a child with emotional dysregulation, and also one of the most important.

There is also a longer arc worth tracking. Boys with ADHD who experience repeated episodes of emotional dysregulation without any framework for understanding them often develop secondary problems: anxiety about losing control, shame about the intensity of their reactions, withdrawal from situations that might trigger an episode. The child who stops signing up for things, who avoids group settings, who preemptively declares he does not care about outcomes, is sometimes a child who has learned that the emotional cost of caring and then being disappointed is too high. Naming the pattern, and naming it without shame, is part of what changes this trajectory.

Working Memory and How It Shapes Every Single Day

Working memory is what allows you to hold information in mind while using it. It is how you keep a grocery list in your head between the time you make it and the time you get to the store. It is how you follow a recipe step by step without reading it again before each step. It is how you track what someone said at the beginning of a conversation while you are formulating your response to the middle of it.

Most people can hold four to seven items in working memory at once and maintain them with reasonable stability over short periods. For a child with ADHD, the capacity is reduced and the stability is unreliable. Items slip out of working memory faster, are displaced more easily by competing stimuli, and have to be re-acquired more often. The child who was told four things on his way upstairs arrives at the top with one or two of them at most, not because he was not listening but because the trace faded before he could act on it.

This is worth sitting with because it reframes so many ordinary conflicts. Your son looks at you while you give him instructions. He nods. He says okay. He goes to do it, and three out of four things do not happen. The gap between "he clearly heard me" and "he clearly did not follow through" looks like willful non-compliance. It is actually the interval between receiving information and acting on it, which for working memory deficits can be enough time for the information to disappear entirely.

The classroom compounds this in specific ways. A teacher who says "open your textbook to page 47, read the first three paragraphs, then answer questions one through four in your notebook" has given a four-step instruction that requires holding all four steps in working memory while executing them in sequence. For a child with intact working memory, this is effortless. For a child with ADHD, by the time he has opened the textbook, he may have retained only that he is supposed to read something and write something, the page number already gone. He opens the book to a random page and starts reading from there. The teacher observes that he is working, does not notice the error, and the assignment is done wrong through a process that looked correct from the outside.

At home, the working memory deficit interacts with time perception in a way that amplifies the difficulty of routines. The morning sequence that requires your son to get dressed, eat breakfast, pack his bag, and be at the door by 7:45 is four things that need to happen in order within a specific time window. Each step requires him to complete the current action, hold the next one in mind, monitor how much time remains, and initiate the transition without external prompting. Each of those sub-tasks draws on a system that is not reliably available to him.

What compensates for unreliable working memory is not more reminders of the same information. It is putting the information in the environment where the action needs to happen, in a format that does not require holding it in mind. A written checklist posted by the door does not need to be remembered. The instruction is still there when the child looks up. A single-step breakdown of a multi-stage task posted in the relevant location means the child never has to hold the whole sequence in mind at once. Each step is visible when needed and does not require retrieval from a storage system that may not be functioning at full capacity. This is not making things easier in a way that removes challenge. It is removing an obstacle that is getting in the way of the actual skill being learned.

Impulsivity as Communication, Not Defiance

When a boy with ADHD blurts out the answer before the teacher has finished asking the question, grabs something off a shelf without checking whether it belongs to someone else, says something sharp and cutting in the middle of an argument before anyone has had time to think, or walks into traffic without looking, the adult response is almost always some version of: why did you do that.

The child's honest answer, when he has one, is: I do not know.

This is not evasion. The deliberation step that normally happens between impulse and action did not occur. The action was out before the part of the brain that evaluates whether to act had time to insert itself into the sequence. From the inside, this feels less like making a bad choice and more like discovering you have already made one. The hand has already reached for the object. The words have already left the mouth. The feet have already crossed the street. The noticing comes after.

Adults respond to impulsive behavior, reasonably enough, by applying consequences. If the child learns that grabbing things leads to consequences, he will stop grabbing things. This logic works for children whose impulse-to-action sequence passes through a deliberation step, because the consequence can be encoded there: do not do this or X will happen. For a child with ADHD, the consequence cannot attach to a step that is not occurring. He knows the rule. He agrees with the rule. He has received the consequence for breaking the rule multiple times. None of that information is available to him in the milliseconds between impulse and action, because those milliseconds are not experienced as decision time.

What consequences can do over time, if applied consistently and without adding shame, is begin to build slower, more deliberate pathways through repeated practice. This is a slow process and it works best in combination with environmental design that reduces the likelihood of triggering situations. What consequences cannot do, at least not quickly, is install a pause mechanism that currently does not exist.

Reading impulsive behavior as communication changes the entire orientation. A boy who starts acting out in the middle of a quiet evening is signaling something about his internal state. Understimulation, because the activity he has been doing for forty minutes has stopped generating the novelty that was keeping him regulated. Physical tension that has been building without an outlet. Low-level anxiety that has reached the threshold where it starts producing behavior rather than staying internal.

The specific form of the impulsivity often points toward the source. Physical impulsivity, running, grabbing, climbing, tends to come from a body that needs movement and sensory input. Verbal impulsivity, blurting, interrupting, saying the thing no one should say, tends to come from a mind that is processing faster than the social situation allows. Social impulsivity, the boundary crossing, the joke that escalates, the touch that is too much, tends to come from a child who stopped tracking the group's cues because his attention had already moved on from the conversation.

None of this means the behavior is acceptable or should go without response. It means the most useful response to impulsive behavior is one that addresses both the behavior and the underlying signal. What happened is the starting point. What was happening inside him right before it happened is the question that leads somewhere useful. One practical implication of this: preventive attention to the conditions your son is in before the impulsivity appears will do more work over time than reactive responses after. If you notice that impulsive behavior tends to cluster at a specific time of day, after school when the decompression from holding it together all day is sudden and complete, or in the late afternoon when stimulant medication is wearing off, or when a particular type of activity has been going on too long without interruption, that pattern is telling you something. The behavior is not random. The triggers are real. Finding them is much more useful than cataloging the incidents.

There is also a social dimension that deserves mention. Boys who are chronically impulsive often have more difficult peer relationships than their ADHD symptoms alone would predict. The child who says the thing that does not need to be said, who pushes too hard in a game, who cannot read the signal to stop, accumulates social costs that compound. He may start being excluded, or included less warmly, in ways he does not fully understand. The experience of social consequence for behavior he does not experience as a choice is one of the more painful aspects of ADHD in boys, and one that does not get discussed as often as the academic challenges.

The Time Blindness Problem and Why Deadlines Feel Abstract

Ask a child with ADHD how long he has been playing video games and he will say fifteen minutes. He has been playing for an hour and forty. Ask him how long his homework will take and he says ten minutes. It takes fifty. Tell him he has thirty minutes before you need to leave for his appointment and he keeps doing what he is doing until you are standing at the door with your keys, already late, visibly frustrated, and he looks genuinely surprised.

This is not carelessness about time. It is a genuine perceptual difference in how time is experienced, and it has a specific name: time blindness. The ADHD brain does not register the passage of time with the same automatic consistency as a neurotypical brain. Most people have something like an internal clock: a background sense of time moving that updates without conscious attention and generates a felt awareness of how long something has been happening and how long remains before a deadline. This clock runs quietly and continuously, which is why most people can feel the difference between ten minutes and twenty-five minutes without looking at a watch, and why a deadline in the future creates a low-level felt urgency that builds as the time approaches. For a child with ADHD, this internal clock is unreliable. Activities that are engaging feel as if they have almost no duration. The child who has been absorbed in something for two hours genuinely experiences it as twenty minutes, not because he is lying or exaggerating but because his sense of time during engagement is compressed in a way that does not match the clock on the wall. Activities that are not engaging feel as if they last forever, which is why sitting through a ten-minute classroom transition can produce the same agitation as a much longer wait in a neurotypical child. The discrepancy between internal time experience and external clock time is consistent and neurological. Deadlines are affected in a specific way. A deadline that is an hour away does not generate a felt sense of urgency because an hour is too abstract to register as real. The experience of the present moment, whatever is happening right now, is vivid and immediate. The experience of the moment an hour from now, including the bus that leaves, the test that starts, the appointment that cannot be moved, is pale and indistinct. It does not compete with the present. It cannot. The felt weight of the future moment has not arrived yet, and for many ADHD kids it does not arrive until the future moment is the present moment, at which point it is often too late. This is why verbal time warnings are so consistently ineffective. "You have twenty minutes" is information about an abstraction. The child hears it, registers the words, and then the information fades quickly because there is no internal mechanism to convert it into a felt countdown. The warning creates no urgency because urgency is not a cognitive response to information about time. It is a felt response, and the mechanism that generates that feeling is not reliably available.

What compensates for this is making time visible and external. A visual timer that the child can see, where the amount remaining is displayed in a format that changes as it decreases, creates an external clock that does not depend on internal perception. The child can see that the red section is smaller than it was ten minutes ago. That visual information reaches him in a way that verbal reminders do not. A timer cube that changes color as time decreases, a sand timer with visible flow, a countdown on a screen placed in the space where he is working: all of these do the same thing. They turn time from an abstraction into something that can be tracked with the eye, without requiring the internal clock to function. The morning rush, the homework procrastination, the last-minute scramble for a project that has been due for a week, the perpetually missed departure times: these are all versions of the same gap. A brain living almost entirely in the present moment, encountering a world that requires consistent projection into the near future. The gap is real and neurological. Closing it requires external structure that provides the time information the internal system cannot reliably generate. That is the practical logic behind every visual schedule, every kitchen timer, every checklist placed at the exact location where the action needs to happen: not accommodation in the sense of lowered expectations, but compensation for a genuine perceptual difference that is not going to be resolved by telling the child to pay more attention to the clock.

Chapter 3: Getting to the Right Diagnosis

Diagnosis is not destiny. It is clarity.

Some parents spend three years circling the question before they get an answer. They have watched their son struggle, heard the same observations repeated at every teacher conference, read everything available about ADHD, and asked a pediatrician about an evaluation more than once. Each time they were told to wait: he is young, boys take longer to settle, give it another year. When the evaluation finally happens, the results confirm what they already knew. The years of waiting were not neutral time. They were years in which he went without support, without accommodation, without a framework that could have made things easier for everyone involved.

Other parents get the diagnosis in a twenty-minute appointment, walk out the door with a label and a prescription and no real understanding of what either one means. They went in with questions and came out with a piece of paper, and now they have to figure out what to do with it on their own, without context, without a plan, without someone to explain the difference between a diagnosis and a direction.

Both experiences are common. Neither one has to define what comes next. What makes the difference is understanding how the diagnostic process actually works: who should conduct it, what a real evaluation looks like, how to prepare your son and yourself, and how to use the results once you have them.

When to Seek an Evaluation and Who to See

The question of when to seek an evaluation often answers itself if you know what to look for. A boy who struggles consistently in school, who receives the same behavioral feedback across multiple teachers and multiple years, who has daily conflicts at home around tasks that require sustained attention or impulse control, who is visibly frustrated by the gap between what he wants to do and what he can manage to do, is showing you through his behavior that something is getting in the way. When those patterns appear across more than one setting and have been present for more than a few months, an evaluation is not a drastic step. It is the logical next move.

The more complicated question is who should conduct the evaluation, and the answer matters more than most parents realize. Several types of professionals are legally authorized to diagnose ADHD, but their training, their tools, and the depth of assessment they provide are not equivalent, and the differences between them have real consequences for the quality of information you walk away with.

Pediatricians can and do diagnose ADHD, particularly for children whose presentation is relatively straightforward. A pediatrician-based evaluation typically involves behavioral rating scales completed by parents and sometimes teachers, a clinical interview, and ruling out medical causes for the symptoms. For some children this level of assessment is sufficient to establish a clear picture and create a working plan. For others it misses important information, particularly when there are co-occurring conditions involved, such as anxiety, learning disabilities, autism spectrum traits, or sensory processing differences that overlap with or complicate the ADHD presentation. A pediatric evaluation that moves quickly toward a diagnosis without exploring what else might be contributing is not necessarily wrong, but it is incomplete, and incomplete information produces incomplete support plans.

Child and adolescent psychiatrists bring more specialized training in complex diagnoses and in the relationship between ADHD and other mental health conditions. If your son has significant emotional difficulties alongside the ADHD symptoms, if he has already had a treatment plan that has not produced the expected results, or if the picture involves medication decisions that feel complicated, a psychiatric evaluation is worth seeking. Psychiatrists are also better positioned to manage medication in cases where the standard approach is not working or where co-occurring conditions create additional considerations.

Neuropsychologists and licensed psychologists who specialize in child assessment conduct the most thorough evaluations available. A full neuropsychological evaluation maps cognitive strengths and weaknesses across multiple domains: attention, working memory, processing speed, executive function, language, visual-spatial reasoning, and academic achievement. It takes several hours spread over one or more sessions and produces a detailed written report that explains not just whether ADHD is present, but what your son's specific cognitive profile looks like and what kinds of support are likely to be most effective for him specifically.

For children whose difficulties are complex, for families who need detailed documentation to access school accommodations, or for situations where the pediatric evaluation has not produced a complete enough picture, this level of assessment is the most useful and the most durable.

When you are choosing a provider, ask about the process before you commit to it. A thorough evaluation involves more than a rating scale and a single appointment. If what is being offered does not include input from the school, does not address the possibility of co-occurring conditions, and does not include any cognitive or academic testing, it is worth asking whether a more comprehensive option is available.

One more thing worth addressing: many parents delay seeking an evaluation because they are worried about labeling their son. This concern is understandable and common. But a label, used correctly, is a description of how a specific brain works. It opens doors to services, accommodations, and understanding that are otherwise closed. A child who goes without a diagnosis is not protected from being labeled; he is labeled anyway, as difficult, as unmotivated, as not trying. The difference is that the informal labels carry blame and the formal one carries a plan.

What a Comprehensive ADHD Assessment Actually Looks Like

A well-conducted ADHD evaluation is not one test. It is a structured process of gathering information from multiple sources and multiple angles, cross-referencing what is found, and systematically ruling out alternative explanations before arriving at a diagnosis. Understanding what the process should include gives you the ability to recognize when something essential is being skipped.

The clinical interview is the foundation. The evaluator spends significant time talking with you about your son's developmental history: when he first started talking and walking, how he did in preschool and early elementary school, what the specific behaviors are that have raised concerns, when those behaviors first appeared, how frequently they occur, which settings they are most pronounced in, and what approaches have already been tried. This conversation should feel substantive, not rushed. The evaluator needs a detailed picture of your son across time and across different contexts to distinguish ADHD from developmental variation, from situational stress, or from other conditions that can look similar.

Behavioral rating scales are completed by multiple people who observe your son in different settings. Typically this means parents and at least one current teacher, sometimes additional school staff or a previous teacher if relevant. These standardized questionnaires measure the frequency and severity of specific behaviors and compare them to samples of children the same age and gender. Rating scales completed only by parents, at home, without teacher input, are not sufficient for a reliable ADHD diagnosis. The diagnostic criteria require that symptoms appear across more than one setting, and establishing that requires data from more than one setting.

Cognitive and academic testing is the backbone of a comprehensive assessment. Intelligence testing measures overall cognitive ability and, critically, reveals significant discrepancies between different cognitive capacities, because a child can score in the superior range for verbal reasoning and in the low average range for working memory, and that discrepancy tells you something important about where the difficulty lives. Academic achievement testing measures actual performance in reading, writing, and math relative to age and grade expectations, which helps identify whether academic struggles are attributable to attention difficulties, to a specific learning disability, or to both.

Attention and executive function measures assess specific capacities such as sustained attention, processing speed, cognitive flexibility, and working memory through standardized tasks. These are distinct from rating scales: they measure what your son can actually do under controlled conditions, rather than what adults observe him doing in natural settings. The combination of performance measures and observational data is more informative than either one alone.

A thorough assessment also includes a medical review to rule out conditions that produce ADHD-like symptoms: sleep disorders, thyroid problems, vision or hearing difficulties, lead exposure, anxiety, and others. Observation data from the classroom or from structured clinic-based activities adds a behavioral layer that questionnaires and tests do not fully capture. Not every evaluation includes direct observation, but when the school report and the home report differ significantly, observation data can clarify which environment is revealing more of the actual pattern.

At the end of this process you should have a clear answer not just to whether your son has ADHD, but to what else may be contributing to his difficulties, what his specific cognitive strengths and weaknesses look like, and what types of support are most likely to help given his particular profile. An evaluation that delivers only a diagnostic label without addressing those questions has not finished the job.

The quality of the evaluation is directly related to the quality of the support plan that follows from it. A rushed assessment that misses a co-occurring learning disability means you will spend months or years working on the wrong problem. The investment in a thorough evaluation, in time and often in cost, pays returns every time someone works with your son from an accurate picture of who he actually is rather than who the brief screening suggested he might be.

How to Prepare Your Son for the Evaluation Process

How you talk to your son about the evaluation will shape how he experiences it, and how he experiences it will shape how he relates to whatever findings come out of it. The preparation is not logistical. It is relational, and it deserves attention before the first appointment.

Most boys, told they are going to see someone who will ask them questions and have them do tasks, want to know two things immediately: am I in trouble, and does something being wrong with me mean I am broken. Both questions are reasonable and both deserve honest, direct answers before the evaluation begins. No, he is not in trouble. And the purpose of the evaluation is not to find out if something is wrong with him but to understand better how his brain works so that the people who care about him can help him in ways that actually work.

The framing you use is the frame he will carry into the room. If the evaluation is presented as a consequence of difficult behavior, or as something that is happening because he is a problem, he will arrive with shame and defensiveness, and the data collected under those conditions will not reflect his actual functioning. If it is presented as a tool for understanding, as something that gives everyone a clearer map of how to help him, he is more likely to engage honestly and produce data that reflects how he actually works.

For younger children, the explanation can be simple: they are going to meet someone who works with kids to help understand how different people think and learn, they will do some activities and answer some questions, it will take a while and there will be breaks, and nothing about it is a test he can pass or fail. For older boys and adolescents, a more direct framing lands better. You have noticed that some things feel harder for him than they seem to for other kids his age, and you want to understand what is behind that so you can actually help him, not just ask him to try harder.

On the practical side, gather everything before the first appointment. Previous school evaluations, report cards from multiple years, teacher comments that have recurred, any behavioral documentation from school, records of previous medical or psychological treatment, and your own observations are all relevant. The more specific your documentation, the more accurate the picture the evaluator can build. A note that says "has always had trouble sitting still" is less useful than "has received the same comments on attention and task completion from five different teachers across four years."

The day before the evaluation, make sure your son is rested and has eaten. Cognitive performance is measurably affected by fatigue and hunger, and a child who is exhausted or hypoglycemic on the day of testing will not show the evaluator what he is capable of. If he takes medication for any condition, continue his regular schedule unless the evaluator specifically asks you to hold it. Prepare him for the length: a comprehensive evaluation is tiring, and a child who knows it will be long and includes scheduled breaks manages the experience differently than one who expected it to be over in an hour.

After the evaluation, however it went, do not debrief him with a long conversation about what the evaluator might have found. Let him know you will talk about it once the results are in. The wait is easier when there is no ambiguity about what he is waiting to hear.

When the results do come in and you are ready to share them with your son, the same framing principles apply. The diagnosis is information. It explains things that have been confusing and hard. It does not change who he is or what he is capable of. Starting that conversation from a place of clarity rather than concern sets the tone for how he will relate to his own diagnosis for years to come.

Understanding the Report and What to Do With It

A full neuropsychological evaluation report runs fifteen to thirty pages and contains enough technical language to feel impenetrable on first read. Most parents read it once, in a state of mild overwhelm, and then file it away. This is a significant missed opportunity, because the report is the most detailed map of your son's cognitive profile that you are likely to have, and learning to navigate it makes it genuinely useful rather than just documentation.

Start with the summary and recommendations section, which typically appears at the end of the report. This section translates the technical findings into plain language and lists specific recommendations for school, home, and any therapeutic interventions the evaluator believes would help. Reading this section first gives you the overall picture before you work through the detailed findings. It also lets you arrive at the score sections already knowing the conclusion, which makes the numbers easier to interpret.

The score sections contain standard scores and percentile ranks. Standard scores compare your son's performance on each measure to the average for his age group. A standard score of 100 represents exactly average performance, with the average range generally defined as scores between 85 and 115. Percentile ranks tell you the percentage of same-age peers your son performed above. A score at the 25th percentile means he performed better than 25 percent of his age group on that measure. What matters most in a neuropsychological profile is not any single number but the pattern across multiple measures: where are the genuine strengths, where are the meaningful gaps, and how do those gaps correspond to the difficulties you observe in daily life.

Pay close attention to any co-occurring conditions identified in the report. Anxiety, dyslexia, processing speed deficits, and autism spectrum traits frequently occur alongside ADHD, and each one changes what effective support looks like. A support plan designed only for ADHD, when there is also an unaddressed reading difficulty or a significant anxiety component, will hit a ceiling and everyone will wonder why the child is not responding as expected. The report should address these possibilities explicitly, not just flag them as considerations.

Once you understand the report, use it actively. Bring it to the school and request a meeting with the student support team to discuss how the findings translate into accommodations and services. The report is the documentation that grounds your son's accommodation requests in clinical evidence. Schools respond more readily to accommodation requests backed by comprehensive evaluation data. Share relevant sections with other professionals working with your son, and keep an updated copy accessible rather than archived.

Schedule a follow-up appointment with the evaluator if one is not already planned. Reading the report on your own is one thing; discussing it with the person who wrote it is another. A good evaluator will walk you through the findings, answer your questions, explain their reasoning on any conclusions that are not clear, and help you prioritize what to do first.

One practical note on sharing the report with your son: the level of detail you share should match his age and readiness. A ten-year-old can understand that the evaluation showed he has ADHD, that his brain is excellent at creative thinking and fast at processing information, and that his working memory, the part of the brain that holds information while you are using it, is an area where he needs extra support. He does not need the percentile ranks or the technical classifications. An older teenager may want to read more of it. Let his curiosity guide how much you share, and be available for questions as they arise rather than presenting everything at once. The report does not expire. It will still be there when he is ready for more of it.

Keep copies organized and accessible. The evaluation report, the school accommodations plan it helped create, notes on what has been tried and what has worked: these documents become a clinical history that any future provider will want to review. Starting that file now, and maintaining it as your son grows and his needs change, is one of the most practical things you can do with the information the evaluation produces.

When You Disagree With the Diagnosis

Sometimes the evaluation produces a conclusion that does not match what you have spent years observing. The evaluator says ADHD when you believe the primary issue is anxiety. Or the report comes back without an ADHD diagnosis when every teacher your son has had for the past five years has raised the same concerns about attention and follow-through. Or the diagnosis feels approximately right but something is missing: a co-occurring condition mentioned in passing and then set aside without adequate exploration. Disagreement in these situations is not denial. It is a clinical signal worth taking seriously.

The most common version of this is a diagnosis that comes back too quickly or too narrowly. A single appointment without teacher rating scales, without cognitive testing, without any exploration of what else might be contributing, has not produced a finding that deserves the confidence it is often given. The issue is not necessarily that the conclusion is wrong, but that the evidence base for it is thin. In this situation the right response is to seek a more thorough evaluation, not to dismiss the existing one, but to supplement it with better data.

A second situation involves evaluations conducted under institutional pressure. Schools sometimes refer children for evaluations with a specific diagnostic outcome in mind because certain diagnoses unlock specific services or resources. An evaluation conducted in that context may be shaped, consciously or not, by what outcome the institution wants. If the evaluation was initiated primarily to satisfy a school eligibility determination and the findings do not align with what you observe at home and what the history suggests, getting an independent evaluation from someone with no relationship to the school is a reasonable and legitimate step.

When you seek a second opinion, you do not need to explain your decision to anyone or frame it as a challenge to the first evaluator. You are entitled to an independent clinical opinion. Find a qualified evaluator, bring all existing documentation including the first report, and be transparent about the fact that a previous evaluation exists and what it found. A good second evaluator will review that report, integrate it with their own findings, and give you their independent clinical impression. Where the two evaluations agree, you have stronger confidence in the conclusion. Where they diverge, you have a meaningful question to investigate further, and that investigation is worth doing. Parental disagreement with a diagnosis, when grounded in careful observation and pursued through appropriate channels, is not obstructionism. Your son cannot advocate for himself across a system that involves evaluators, school teams, physicians, and treatment providers. You are the only person who sees the full picture across all of those contexts. When the diagnosis does not fit the full picture, trusting that instinct and pursuing better information is not just reasonable. It is the job.

One thing that can help when navigating disagreement is documentation. If you believe a diagnosis is incomplete or inaccurate, write down specifically what does not fit and why. Which behaviors the diagnosis does not account for. Which observations are inconsistent with the diagnostic profile. Which situations the current plan does not address. This kind of specificity turns a general discomfort into a productive clinical conversation. An evaluator or treating physician who hears concrete, observed behavioral data is in a different conversation than one who hears general skepticism. Disagreement also does not have to be all-or-nothing. A diagnosis can be broadly correct while still being incomplete. Accepting the ADHD diagnosis while continuing to advocate for investigation of a co-occurring anxiety disorder, for example, is not contradictory. The diagnostic process is iterative, and a good clinician expects the picture to sharpen over time as more is learned about how your son responds to various interventions.

Chapter 4:
The Medication Question

The goal of medication is not to change your child. It is to help your child access who they already are.

No decision in ADHD parenting carries more emotional weight than the medication question. Parents who have just received a diagnosis often describe it as the moment everything splits into before and after: before, there was a problem without a name; after, there is a name and a treatment conversation that many were not prepared for.

The fear is understandable. Giving a child medication, particularly a stimulant medication, runs against a deeply ingrained instinct that says a child's brain should be left alone to develop on its own. The worry about dependency, about long-term effects, about changing something essential about who your son is: these are not irrational concerns. They are what responsible parents feel when facing a decision with real stakes.

At the same time, parents who have watched their son struggle for years, and who have tried every behavioral approach available, often arrive at the medication conversation from the opposite direction: not fear of trying it, but exhaustion from not having tried it while everything else has failed to produce sustained change.

Neither position is wrong. What they both need is the same thing: accurate information, stripped of the mythology that surrounds this topic in both directions. This chapter is not here to tell you what to decide. It is here to make sure that whatever you decide, you are deciding from a clear understanding of what the evidence actually says.

What Parents Need to Know Before Deciding

The first thing to know is that stimulant medications for ADHD are the most thoroughly studied treatments in the history of child psychiatry. Methylphenidate, the active ingredient in medications like Ritalin, Concerta, and Methylin, has been in continuous use and continuous study since the 1950s.

Amphetamine-based medications, including Adderall and Vyvanse, have a comparably long research history. There is no other treatment in pediatric medicine with a larger body of evidence supporting its effectiveness, and the effectiveness rates across that body of research are consistently high: approximately 70 to 80 percent of children with ADHD show meaningful improvement in attention and behavior when placed on an appropriately titrated stimulant medication.

That number matters because it puts the medication question in context. This is not a trial treatment with uncertain outcomes. For most children, medication works, and works substantially. The question is not whether it works in general but whether it will work for your son specifically, and what the full picture looks like in his case.

The fear of dependency is one of the most common reasons parents hesitate, and it deserves a direct answer. Stimulant medications used at therapeutic doses for ADHD do not produce the kind of dependency seen with recreational stimulant use. The doses involved are calibrated to address a neurological deficit, not to produce the euphoric effect associated with misuse. Research on long-term outcomes has consistently found that children with ADHD who receive appropriate medication treatment are not at higher risk of developing substance use problems in adolescence or adulthood. Some studies suggest the opposite pattern: untreated ADHD, with its associated frustration, impulsivity, and risk-taking behavior, correlates with higher rates of substance use. Medication that reduces those drivers may reduce that risk.

The concern about effects on growth is real and worth monitoring, not dismissing. Some children on stimulant medications experience reduced appetite, which can affect weight and, over extended periods, height. This effect is typically modest, is more pronounced in the early months of treatment, and tends to diminish over time. It is also manageable: timing medications strategically around meals, ensuring adequate caloric intake in the morning before the medication takes full effect, and discussing the concern openly with the prescribing physician are all practical responses. It is a side effect worth tracking, not a reason to avoid treatment.

The concern about personality change is where parents most often feel the gap between what they feared and what they see. Some children do become quieter on medication than they were before, and this can alarm parents who interpret quieter as less themselves. The distinction that matters is between a child who is quieter because the impulsive output has decreased and a child who seems emotionally flat and robotic. The first is usually what medication is supposed to produce. The second is a signal that the dose is too high or the medication is the wrong fit. The goal, stated precisely, is a child who can sit still and focus without losing the spark that makes him who he is. If that is not what you are seeing, the medication adjustment conversation with the doctor needs to happen.

One more thing worth naming before the decision is made: the social and relational costs of untreated ADHD are real and they accumulate. A child who is struggling daily with attention, impulse control, and emotional regulation is not simply having a harder time at school. He is building a self-concept from years of feedback that tells him he is difficult, undependable, or not smart enough. He is straining the relationships with peers and adults that matter for his development. He may be developing anxiety or depression as secondary conditions layered on top of the primary one. The question is never just "what are the risks of medication" in isolation. It is "what are the costs of this specific level of impairment continuing, and what are the costs of treating it." Both sides of that comparison deserve honest assessment.

The decision to try medication is also not permanent. It is the beginning of a structured observation process. If the results are not what you hoped, the medication can be stopped. If the side effects are not manageable, the approach can change. Starting is not committing to a lifetime outcome. It is generating information about your son's specific neurological response to a specific treatment, and that information, whatever it turns out to be, is useful.

The Main Types of ADHD Medication and How They Work

ADHD medications fall into two main categories: stimulants and non-stimulants. Stimulants are the first-line treatment for most children and the most effective across the population. Non-stimulants are a second-line option for children who do not respond to stimulants, cannot tolerate them, or have co-occurring conditions that make stimulants a less appropriate choice.

Within the stimulant category, there are two chemical families: methylphenidate and amphetamine. These are different molecules that act on overlapping but not identical neural pathways. A child who does not respond well to one family may respond well to the other, which is why treatment trials often involve trying both before concluding that stimulants are not a good fit. Within each family, there are short-acting and long-acting formulations. Short-acting versions last three to four hours and require a midday dose, which can be logistically complicated and creates a visible reminder of the medication at school. Long-acting versions are designed to last six to twelve hours, covering the school day and early evening without a midday dose. Most prescribers start with a long-acting formulation for this reason, though short-acting versions remain useful as supplements to cover specific windows not reached by the longer formulation.

Methylphenidate-based long-acting medications include Concerta, Ritalin LA, Metadate CD, and several generic equivalents. The mechanisms of delivery differ between formulations, which affects the timing and smoothness of the effect curve. Concerta, for example, uses a pump delivery system designed to maintain relatively steady medication levels across the day without a pronounced spike and drop. Amphetamine-based long-acting options include Adderall XR, Vyvanse, and Mydayis, among others. Vyvanse is a prodrug, meaning it is converted to active amphetamine in the body after ingestion, which produces a particularly smooth onset and avoids the abrupt effects sometimes associated with immediate-release formulations.

Non-stimulant options include atomoxetine, sold under the brand name Strattera, and alpha-2 agonists including guanfacine and clonidine. Atomoxetine is a selective norepinephrine reuptake inhibitor that affects attention regulation through a different pathway than stimulants. It takes four to six weeks to reach full effect, which is a significant difference from stimulants that produce noticeable effects within hours. This slower timeline makes it less useful for quickly assessing fit, but it is a valid option for children with significant anxiety alongside ADHD or those who have not tolerated stimulants. Guanfacine and clonidine work differently again, primarily through noradrenergic pathways, and are often used in combination with stimulants to address specific symptoms like hyperactivity, impulsivity, and sleep difficulties, or as alternatives when stimulants are contraindicated.

The mechanism underlying all stimulant treatment is an increase in the availability of dopamine and norepinephrine in the prefrontal cortex, the region responsible for executive function. This is not adding something foreign to the brain. It is supplementing a system that is not producing adequate concentrations of these neurotransmitters to support consistent self-regulation. When the system is appropriately supplemented, the management layer of the brain becomes more reliable, and the activation problems that produce the observable ADHD behaviors decrease.

In practical terms, what this means for the titration process is important to understand. Finding the right medication and dose for a specific child is rarely accomplished at the first appointment. The standard process involves starting at a conservative dose, observing the response over one to two weeks across multiple settings, reporting what was observed to the physician, and then adjusting upward or changing formulations based on that report. This cycle repeats until a therapeutic dose is established: one that produces meaningful improvement in function with tolerable side effects. For most children this process takes two to three months. For some it takes longer, particularly if the first medication family tried is not a good fit and the trial moves to the second family. Planning for this timeline from the start prevents the premature conclusion that medication is not working when what is actually happening is that the right dose has not yet been found.

The time of day when medication takes effect is also a practical consideration that affects daily life. A long-acting stimulant taken at seven in the morning typically begins producing its effect within thirty to sixty minutes, reaches peak effect in the late morning, and diminishes through the afternoon. This curve means that school hours are usually well-covered. The period after school, when a child is home and medication is wearing off, is often the most behaviorally challenging time of day regardless of whether medication is involved. Understanding this pattern helps parents set appropriate expectations for what the school day will look like versus what the evening at home will look like.

Working Effectively With Your Son's Doctor

The prescribing physician is a partner in a process, not the authority who hands down decisions. Understanding this from the start makes the relationship significantly more effective.

The prescribing doctor has clinical training and access to research. You have continuous, granular observational data about your son across multiple settings and over extended time. Neither of those inputs alone is sufficient to make good medication decisions. Together they are. The doctor needs what you observe. You need what the doctor knows. The partnership works when both parties treat their contribution as essential.

Before starting any new medication or adjusting a current one, establish what you are measuring and how. This sounds clinical but it does not need to be complicated. A brief daily rating of attention, impulse control, and emotional regulation, scored on a simple scale and noted in a consistent location, gives you data you can bring to the follow-up appointment rather than an impression. The difference between "I think things got a little better" and "his teacher and I both rated his ability to stay on task significantly higher in weeks two and three compared to baseline, but we noticed increased irritability after school starting in week two" is not just precision. It is the kind of information that allows the doctor to make targeted adjustments.

At each appointment, come prepared with specific observations, not just general impressions. When does the medication seem most effective? When does it seem to wear off? Are there specific times of day when the symptoms are more pronounced? What side effects have you noticed, and when do they appear relative to the dose timing? Are there situations at school or home where you have seen clear improvement? Are there situations where the improvement you hoped for has not appeared?

Questions worth asking at every medication appointment include: Is the current dose achieving what we hoped? Are the side effects we are seeing typical or worth addressing directly? Is it time to consider a dose adjustment, a formulation change, or an additional medication to address specific gaps? What should prompt me to call before the next scheduled appointment?

The six-month check-in model is not adequate for medication management, particularly in the early phases of treatment when finding the right medication and dose involves multiple small adjustments. Monthly appointments in the first several months, with a clear protocol for contacting the office between appointments if something unexpected happens, is a more appropriate cadence. Once things are stable and working well, the monitoring interval can extend. But stable and working well is a conclusion that needs to be earned, not assumed.

One practical tool that dramatically improves the quality of medication appointments is a simple behavioral log kept by both the parent and the teacher. This does not need to be elaborate. A brief daily rating on three to five dimensions, such as attention at tasks, impulse control, emotional regulation, appetite, and sleep, gives the physician something to work with that is far more useful than retrospective impressions. Many prescribers provide their own rating scales for this purpose. If yours does not, the Vanderbilt Assessment Scale, which is widely available online, serves the same function and is specifically designed for tracking ADHD symptoms and medication effects over time.

Communication with the school is equally important in the medication monitoring process. Teachers see your son for six or more hours a day under structured conditions that are directly relevant to what medication is supposed to address. Their observations are clinical data. A teacher who reports that the child's ability to stay on task has improved substantially since starting medication is providing information you cannot gather at home. A teacher who reports that the child seems subdued and unlike himself is providing a different but equally important signal. Establishing a brief communication channel with the primary teacher when a medication trial is starting, and explicitly asking for their observations over the following weeks, makes the information flow automatic rather than something you have to remember to pursue.

Monitoring Effects and Knowing When to Adjust

Starting a new medication or adjusting a dose is not a one-time event. It is the beginning of an observation window. Knowing what to look for, and how to distinguish a good response from a partial response from a problematic response, is the practical skill that makes the difference between medication management that works and medication management that drifts.

In the first week or two after starting a new medication, watch for three things: signs of positive effect, signs of side effects, and the timing of both. Positive effects in ADHD medication typically include improved ability to sustain attention on tasks that previously produced rapid drift, reduced impulsive behavior during structured activities, a child who can get through homework without the escalation that was previously typical, and sometimes improved emotional regulation and reduced reactivity. These effects, when they appear, are usually noticeable. Teachers often comment without being prompted. The child sometimes notices himself.

Side effects to watch for with stimulant medications include appetite suppression, particularly around lunchtime; difficulty falling asleep if the medication is still active at bedtime; irritability or emotional sensitivity, sometimes called rebound, as the medication wears off in the late afternoon; and a flattening of personality or affect that suggests the dose may be higher than necessary. Not every child experiences all of these, and most side effects are manageable through timing adjustments or dose modifications rather than medication changes. But you need to observe them accurately to report them to the physician, and accurate observation requires that you and the teacher are both paying attention and communicating.

The rebound effect deserves specific attention because it is one of the most commonly misunderstood phenomena in ADHD medication management. As a stimulant medication wears off, some children experience a temporary intensification of ADHD symptoms that can be worse than their baseline. The child who was calm and focused through the school day arrives home and falls apart completely in the first hour. This is not evidence that the medication is making things worse overall. It is a pharmacological pattern associated with the dopamine regulation cycle. Options for managing it include adjusting the timing of the long-acting dose, adding a small dose of short-acting medication in the late afternoon to smooth the transition, or switching to a formulation with a different release curve.

Sleep problems deserve particular attention because they interact with ADHD symptoms in a circular way. Many children with ADHD already have difficulty falling asleep as part of their neurological profile, independent of medication. Stimulant medications that extend late into the evening can amplify this pre-existing difficulty. The result is a child who is not getting adequate sleep, which directly worsens attention and emotional regulation the next day, which can be misread as inadequate medication effect and prompt a dose increase, which further disrupts sleep. If your son is having significant sleep difficulties, report it early and specifically: what time he takes his medication, what time he starts trying to fall asleep, what time he is actually falling asleep, and what the sleep quality looks like. The physician may recommend adjusting the timing of the dose, switching to a formulation with a shorter duration, or adding a low-dose sleep support to bridge the evening transition.

Keeping a consistent written log through all of this is not excessive. It is the difference between navigating by memory, which is unreliable over the weeks and months that medication adjustment takes, and navigating by data, which allows you to see patterns that are not visible day to day. A simple note of medication timing, dose, and one or two behavioral observations per day takes two minutes and produces the kind of longitudinal information that makes every appointment with the physician more productive.

The question of medication holidays, stopping medication on weekends, school breaks, or summers, comes up in most ADHD medication conversations. There is no universally correct answer. Some families use medication breaks to give the child's appetite and growth a recovery window, and to establish a clearer baseline of how he is functioning without it. Other families find that the benefits of medication extend beyond school performance to family life, social interactions, and emotional regulation in ways that make discontinuing on weekends counterproductive. This is a decision to make collaboratively with the physician based on your son's specific profile, how he functions off medication, and what the goals of treatment are.

When Medication Is Not Enough on Its Own

Medication improves the signal. It does not teach the skills that were never learned because the signal was always too noisy to receive them clearly.

A child who has spent five years in school with dysregulated attention and impulsivity has not been building the same organizational skills, study habits, and self-monitoring strategies that his peers were assembling during those same years. When medication makes sustained attention more available, those missing skills do not appear automatically. They need to be taught, practiced, and reinforced over time, in a brain that can now receive that instruction more reliably than it could before. Medication creates the conditions for learning. It does not substitute for learning.

Executive function skills are among the most important gaps to address alongside medication. Task initiation, organization, time management, working memory strategies, and emotional regulation: each of these can be developed through specific coaching and practice, and the effectiveness of that work is substantially higher when medication provides a more stable neurological platform. This is one of the strongest arguments for a combined treatment approach: the combination of medication and behavioral skills training produces better long-term outcomes than either one alone, because the skills built during treatment persist even when medication is adjusted or discontinued.

Social skills are another domain where medication alone rarely produces the results parents hope for. A child whose impulsivity has produced years of friction with peers, who has accumulated a reputation for going too far or not reading the room, who has learned to withdraw from social situations to avoid the unpredictability of his own reactions, is not going to rebuild those patterns simply because medication has reduced the impulsivity. The relational damage and the learned avoidance need direct attention, through social skills groups, through coaching specific to his relationship patterns, and through deliberate construction of positive social experiences in manageable settings.

Anxiety, which co-occurs with ADHD in a significant proportion of children, is another dimension that medication alone does not address and can sometimes worsen. Stimulant medications that increase arousal can amplify existing anxiety in some children, making a targeted anxiety intervention, whether behavioral, therapeutic, or pharmacological, a necessary part of the overall plan. Missing this because everything is attributed to ADHD and medication is expected to cover it leads to incomplete improvement and often to a parent concluding that medication has failed, when what has actually happened is that a second condition was not treated.

Parent training is another component that consistently shows up in the research on combined treatment for ADHD. Not parent training in the sense of learning to be stricter or more consistent, but in the sense of learning specific behavioral management strategies that are matched to how ADHD brains work. Techniques like effective command-giving, structured reward systems calibrated to short time horizons, planned ignoring of minor misbehavior that competes with positive reinforcement, and predictable transition protocols produce measurably better outcomes when parents learn and apply them systematically. Programs based on Russell Barkley's parent training model, or similar evidence-based curricula, are available through many therapists and parent training centers. The investment of time in learning these approaches pays returns every day, across every challenging interaction.

For boys specifically, physical activity is a behavioral intervention that is often underutilized because it does not look like therapy. Regular vigorous exercise, particularly aerobic activity, has documented effects on dopamine and norepinephrine levels in the prefrontal cortex that overlap meaningfully with the effects of stimulant medication. It does not replace medication for most children, but it is a genuine neurological support that complements everything else in the treatment plan. A boy who has sixty minutes of physically demanding exercise daily, in a form he actually enjoys, is not just healthier. He is running on a more available neurological substrate for everything you are trying to build.

The most accurate metaphor for medication in the overall treatment picture is that it opens a window. When the window is open, the child is more accessible to everything you are trying to do: the structure you are building at home, the support the school is providing, the coaching or therapy he is receiving, the relationship you are working to protect. The window being open does not do any of those things for you. It just makes them possible in a way they were not before. What you build during that time is what carries forward.

Chapter 5:
Sleep, Food, and the Body-Brain Connection

Sleep is the single most effective thing we can do to reset our brain and body health each day.

It is eleven at night. Your son is still awake. Not playing, not on a screen, just lying in the dark with his mind continuing to run at a speed that does not match the hour. You have said goodnight twice. You have checked on him. He is not trying to stay up. He is simply unable to fall asleep, and the expression on his face when you look in is not defiance. It is something closer to frustration, maybe even embarrassment, that his body is not doing the thing everyone else seems to do without effort.

Tomorrow will be harder than today was. A child with ADHD who is also sleep-deprived is running a significant additional deficit on top of everything the ADHD already costs him. Every symptom, attention, impulse control, emotional regulation, time perception, is meaningfully worsened by inadequate sleep, and the worsening is not subtle. A bad night for a typical child means a slow morning. A bad night for a child with ADHD can mean a day that looks like an entirely different child.

The body is not separate from the ADHD brain. It is part of the same system. Sleep patterns, eating patterns, hydration, and physical wellness all feed directly into the neurological substrate that shapes how well your son can function on any given day. This chapter is about understanding that connection clearly enough to actually do something with it.

Why ADHD Boys Struggle to Wind Down at Night

The difficulty falling asleep that many children with ADHD experience is not, in most cases, a behavioral problem. It is a neurological one, and treating it like a behavioral problem produces conflict without producing sleep.

One of the most consistent findings in ADHD research is a delay in circadian rhythm, the biological clock that regulates when the body initiates sleep. In the general population, the natural melatonin peak, the surge of the hormone that signals the brain to begin sleep preparation, occurs in the early to mid-evening. In many people with ADHD, this peak is shifted one to two hours later. A child with ADHD who is told to go to bed at nine may be lying there while his biological clock is still signaling that it is mid-evening. The darkness, the quiet instructions to sleep, none of that overrides a hormonal clock that has not yet reached its natural threshold. He is not refusing to cooperate. He is genuinely not ready, in a way that is physiological rather than behavioral.

This circadian delay is one reason why strict enforcement of early bedtimes often makes things worse rather than better. A child whose melatonin peak naturally arrives at ten-thirty, placed in bed at eight-thirty and told to sleep, will spend two hours in a state of increasing frustration. The parent interprets this as resistance. The child experiences it as being asked to do something his body genuinely cannot do yet. Both of them are right about what they are observing. Neither is wrong. The mismatch is between the social expectation of an appropriate bedtime and the biological reality of a clock running late.

The second piece of the sleep difficulty is the state of the central nervous system at day's end. A child with ADHD has typically spent the day managing significant amounts of stimulation: the sensory load of a classroom, the social demands of peer interaction, the cognitive effort of suppressing impulses and tracking transitions, and often a full complement of emotional events, corrections, frustrations, and conflicts. The regulatory system that handles all of this input does not switch off instantly when the school day ends or when the house goes quiet. It continues running, discharging, and processing in ways that keep the nervous system in a state of low-level activation that is genuinely incompatible with sleep onset.

The result is a child who is tired but cannot fall asleep. The tiredness is real. The inability to sleep is equally real. In ADHD, these two states coexist regularly, and the combination is harder to address than either one alone. An overtired child who has not yet downregulated will often become more activated as the evening progresses, not less. Fatigue in an underregulated nervous system can paradoxically increase arousal, which is why parents sometimes see their son become more energetic and harder to settle at nine or ten at night even after a full day. This is not performance or manipulation. It is a nervous system that has not yet found its way back to baseline.

The practical consequence is that wind-down needs to start earlier than parents typically think, and what happens in the hour before bed matters far less than what happens in the two hours before that. Reducing stimulation, transitioning away from conflict and high-energy activity, moving toward quieter and more predictable conditions: this preparation needs to begin well before the targeted sleep time to give the nervous system enough runway to actually slow down. An hour of low-stimulation activity is not always sufficient. The child who went from a homework argument to a thirty-minute wind-down routine and then to bed will not be as ready for sleep as the child whose evening was calm for two hours.

Understanding the neurological basis of this difficulty also changes what is worth fighting about. Insisting on lights-out at nine when your son's circadian clock is not ready until eleven will produce two hours of enforcement work every night, with the child getting little sleep and both of you ending the day in conflict. Working with the biology, which may mean a temporarily later bedtime combined with consistent morning wake times and careful light management to gradually shift the circadian window earlier, often produces more sleep with less conflict. The goal is a child who is actually asleep, not one who is technically in bed at the right time.

Building a Sleep Routine That Actually Works

A sleep routine is not a checklist to be completed before bed. It is a biological signal that teaches the brain, through consistent repetition, that a particular sequence of events precedes sleep. The signal works because it is reliable. A routine that happens at approximately the same time in approximately the same order sends a consistent message. A routine that varies from night to night, is skipped when things run late, or is enforced only when a parent has energy to enforce it, does not develop into a signal. It remains a set of tasks.

The most impactful single variable in a sleep routine for a child with ADHD is light. Blue-spectrum light, the kind produced by screens, LED lighting, and most modern overhead bulbs, suppresses melatonin production by signaling to the brain that it is still daytime. For a child whose melatonin production is already delayed, additional blue light in the evening pushes the sleep window even later. Shifting to warm-spectrum bulbs in the bedroom and living areas after dinner, reducing or eliminating screen use in the sixty to ninety minutes before bed, and using amber or red night lights when light is needed are all changes with direct effects on how quickly sleep onset arrives. This is not a lifestyle preference. It is working with the same hormonal mechanism that makes staying awake easier on summer evenings and harder in winter.

Temperature is underused as a sleep lever. The body initiates sleep most efficiently when core temperature is slightly declining. A room that is too warm keeps the thermoregulatory system active in a way that interferes with sleep onset. Most sleep researchers identify the sixty-five to sixty-eight degree Fahrenheit range as optimal for most people. For families without climate control or in warmer climates, a fan directed at the sleeping area, a slightly cooler shower before bed, or switching to lighter bedding approximates the same effect. Small adjustments in room temperature can produce noticeably faster sleep onset in children who otherwise lie awake for an extended period.

The structure of the pre-sleep sequence should be simple enough that the child can run it with minimal adult direction. A routine that requires active parental management of every step does not build the self-regulating capacity that transfers to the teenage years, when your ability to manage the routine will be significantly reduced. A sequence of three or four steps that the child can initiate and complete independently, such as a shower or bath, changing into pajamas, brushing teeth, and fifteen minutes of reading or a quiet non-screen activity in a dim room, becomes a genuine sleep-initiation pattern when practiced consistently enough. The parent's role is to ensure the conditions are set, not to supervise each transition.

The two forms of resistance that appear most often are the child who insists he is not tired and the child who gets into bed and repeatedly comes back out. For the child who insists he is not tired, the reframe that actually works is changing the objective: the goal is not to fall asleep immediately, but to lie still in a quiet, dark room and allow the body the opportunity to begin sleep. Sleep usually follows. The body does not need to be told to sleep when the conditions are right. It needs to be given the conditions. For the child who repeatedly gets up, the most effective response is a calm, brief, and identical return to bed each time, with no extended conversation, no negotiation, and no escalation. The engagement itself is stimulating and counterproductive. Neutrality and consistency produce results that escalation does not.

When sleep difficulties are chronic and the circadian delay pattern is pronounced, low-dose melatonin is worth discussing with the prescribing physician. Melatonin is not a sedative and does not produce dependency. It is a signaling molecule that communicates to the brain that it is time to begin sleep preparation. Used at the right time in the evening, typically ninety minutes to two hours before the desired sleep time rather than immediately before bed, it can help shift the circadian window to an earlier hour. It is not a substitute for a consistent routine, but for children with significant circadian delay it can meaningfully close the gap between when the family needs sleep to happen and when the child's biology is actually ready for it.

How Nutrition Affects Focus and Behavior

The relationship between what a child eats and how his brain performs is more direct than most parents expect, and less dramatic than the nutritional mythology surrounding ADHD tends to suggest. The mechanism is not complicated. The brain requires a consistent supply of glucose to function. When that supply is stable across the day, cognitive performance is steadier. When it fluctuates sharply, cognitive performance fluctuates with it, and the fluctuations show up most visibly in the capacities that are already most challenged: attention, impulse control, and emotional regulation.

Breakfast is the clearest example of this dynamic and the one with the most direct daily consequences. A child who skips breakfast, or eats only a rapidly digested carbohydrate such as a bowl of sweetened cereal or a piece of white toast, starts the school day with a blood glucose spike followed by a drop that arrives somewhere around nine or ten in the morning. That drop in blood glucose produces difficulty concentrating, increased irritability, and reduced impulse control, all of which look exactly like ADHD symptoms worsening. In a child who already has ADHD, the glucose drop adds a second deficit on top of the neurological one he started with. The result at mid-morning can look like a significant deterioration that neither the teacher nor the parent can explain, because no one is tracking what the child ate three hours earlier.

A breakfast that includes protein and fat alongside carbohydrates produces a much slower and more stable glucose release across the morning. Eggs with toast, Greek yogurt with fruit, oatmeal with nut butter, peanut butter on whole grain bread: all of these options sustain blood glucose through the mid-morning period in a way that a purely carbohydrate breakfast does not. This does not require elaborate preparation or a change in family food culture. It requires understanding that the composition of breakfast has a measurable effect on what the brain is doing two hours later, and making a few substitutions accordingly.

The same principle applies throughout the day. Long gaps between eating produce blood glucose dips that worsen every ADHD symptom. A child who eats lunch at eleven-thirty and has nothing again until dinner at six is running on declining fuel through the entire after-school period, which is already the most challenging window of the day for children on stimulant medication as the dose begins to wear off. A small afternoon snack that includes protein, some cheese, a handful of nuts, hummus with crackers, can change the entire character of the four to six o'clock hours in ways that are significant both for the child's regulation and for the parent's experience of managing him.

Appetite suppression from stimulant medication creates a practical complication for many families. A child who has little appetite during the peak hours of medication effect may resist eating at the times when nutrition is most needed. The strategies that work best for this include a full breakfast before the medication takes effect, a smaller and more flexible mid-day meal when appetite is genuinely limited, and a larger dinner once the medication has largely cleared and appetite has returned naturally. For the period of peak appetite suppression, calorie-dense options that require little appetite to consume, a smoothie with protein powder or nut butter, a handful of trail mix, full-fat yogurt, can maintain adequate nutrition without turning every meal into a negotiation.

One observational practice that many parents find useful is tracking the correlation between meal timing and composition and the behavioral patterns that follow over the course of a few days. The child who is consistently most dysregulated between four and six may be the child who has not eaten since noon. The child who has the most difficult mornings may be eating a breakfast that does not sustain him. Making these connections visible, even informally, shifts the question from why is he always like this at this time to what does he need physically at this time, and that second question has actionable answers.

Sugar, Additives, and What the Research Actually Shows

The belief that sugar causes or significantly amplifies ADHD symptoms is among the most persistent pieces of nutritional folklore in child health, and it does not hold up to scrutiny. Controlled double-blind studies conducted since the 1980s have consistently failed to find a causal relationship between sugar consumption and increased ADHD symptoms. In the most cited of these studies, children given sugar performed no differently on behavioral measures than children given a placebo, even when their parents believed they had consumed sugar. Meta-analyses pooling multiple studies reach the same conclusion. The sugar hypothesis was widely believed and plausible-sounding, but careful testing has not supported it.

What is worth distinguishing from this finding is the effect of blood glucose instability on behavior and attention, which is real and measurable regardless of ADHD status. The problem is not the sugar molecule itself. It is the pattern of eating that produces sharp rises and falls in blood glucose, which often includes high-sugar foods but is not limited to them. A large serving of white rice, a plain bagel, or a bowl of refined pasta can produce a similar glycemic response to a candy bar, depending on what else is consumed with it. Eliminating sugar while continuing to eat in patterns that create glycemic swings will not solve the underlying problem. The relevant variable is glucose stability across the day, not sugar in isolation.

Artificial food colorings and preservatives represent a more genuinely contested area. The most frequently cited evidence is a 2007 study published in The Lancet that found a mixture of artificial colorings and sodium benzoate, a common preservative, increased hyperactivity in children regardless of ADHD diagnosis. The finding prompted regulatory action in several countries and influenced food labeling requirements in the European Union. Subsequent research has been less consistent. Some studies replicate the effect, others do not. Current regulatory positions vary significantly by country, which reflects the genuine uncertainty in the evidence base rather than negligence on anyone's part.

The practical position that most clinicians take is not to recommend sweeping dietary eliminations based on the general concern about food additives, but to encourage careful observation of whether specific foods or eating patterns are associated with specific behavioral changes in your individual son. Children with ADHD do not all respond to food additives the same way. Some parents notice clear patterns. Others observe no connection at all. If you have noticed that your son's behavior is consistently different after consuming particular foods, that observation is worth investigating with his physician rather than either dismissing or acting on independently. If you have not noticed a consistent pattern, there is no strong evidence-based reason to impose restrictive dietary rules that create social difficulty and family conflict without a corresponding benefit.

Omega-3 fatty acids deserve specific mention because they represent the one nutritional intervention with a genuine and replicated evidence base for ADHD.

Multiple individual studies and several formal meta-analyses have found modest but consistent benefits of combined EPA and DHA supplementation on attention, impulse control, and to a lesser extent hyperactivity in children with ADHD. The effect sizes are smaller than those produced by stimulant medication, and the research is not uniformly positive, but the findings are consistent enough across different research groups that most clinicians who follow the literature view omega-3 supplementation as a reasonable low-risk adjunct to the primary treatment approach rather than an unproven fringe intervention. Fish oil providing both EPA and DHA is the most studied delivery form. The supplement does not replace medication for children who need it, and it does not produce dramatic results on its own. What it does, in children who respond to it, is provide a modest baseline improvement that can contribute to the overall picture.

The broader principle worth carrying from this section is that nutrition affects the ADHD brain without curing it. No dietary intervention will replace evidence-based treatment. What dietary attention will do is reduce the number of additional variables that are making an already challenging neurological situation harder. A child who is nutritionally supported is not a child without ADHD. He is a child whose ADHD is operating without the added burden of blood glucose instability, micronutrient deficiency, or the specific sensitivities that some children genuinely have to certain food components. That is a meaningful difference even when it is not a dramatic one.

The Role of Hydration and Physical Wellness

The connection between hydration and cognitive function is one of the most consistently documented and consistently underestimated findings in pediatric health research. Mild dehydration, meaning a fluid deficit of as little as one to two percent of body weight, produces measurable decrements in attention, working memory, and mood in children. The magnitude of the effect is not trivial. Studies that have compared cognitive performance in mildly dehydrated children against the same children adequately hydrated have found differences that are visible on standard neuropsychological measures. For a child whose attention and working memory are already compromised by ADHD, an additional decrement from dehydration is compounding an existing difficulty rather than creating a new one.

The specific challenge in ADHD is that many children with the condition do not reliably register thirst as a cue to drink. Interoception, the capacity to accurately perceive internal body states, is often less dependable in ADHD brains than in neurotypical ones. A child may be meaningfully thirsty without receiving or processing the signal with enough clarity to act on it. He is not ignoring thirst. The signal is not reaching him reliably. The result is a child who goes from breakfast to lunch without drinking anything, not because he refused opportunities to drink but because he never felt the prompt that would lead him to seek them out.

The practical solution is environmental rather than motivational. A water bottle that accompanies your son throughout the day, refilled consistently rather than left to run empty and get forgotten, creates an opportunity for hydration that does not depend on him initiating it from an internal cue. Pairing drinking with predictable daily anchors, before sitting down to homework, before leaving the house in the morning, with every meal and snack, turns hydration into a habit triggered by external structure rather than something that depends on interoception. This is the same principle that works for every other executive function challenge in ADHD: make the desired behavior happen through design rather than through internal self-regulation, because the internal system is not reliably available for this kind of monitoring.

Physical wellness more broadly is a variable that parents frequently underestimate when trying to understand variations in their son's behavior. Illness affects the ADHD brain disproportionately. A child fighting off a mild virus, experiencing low-level pain from an ear infection, dental issue, or persistent headache, or in the early stages of an illness before clear symptoms emerge, is running at reduced neurological capacity in a way that amplifies every ADHD symptom. A day that seems inexplicably worse than the days surrounding it is sometimes a day when the child's system is under physical stress that has not yet surfaced visibly. Before attributing a bad day to a regression or a new problem, it is worth asking whether anything physical might be affecting him.

Sensory experience also belongs in this category. A child who is processing excessive sensory input throughout the day, a noisy classroom with hard surfaces, fluorescent lighting that flickers, the texture of certain clothing, a cafeteria that is overwhelming at full volume, is spending cognitive and regulatory resources on sensory management that are then unavailable for attention and impulse control. The child who is under-stimulated sensorially is seeking input through movement and restlessness in ways that look like hyperactivity but are actually a regulatory need. Neither state is voluntary. Both are physiological. Noticing where your son sits on the sensory spectrum on any given day, what environments support his regulation and which ones deplete it, gives you information that is directly actionable in how you structure his home environment and in what you advocate for in his school placement.

The unifying idea across all of this is straightforward: every variable that affects physical wellbeing, sleep, nutrition, hydration, illness, sensory load, feeds into the same neurological substrate that ADHD is already stressing. None of these factors operates independently. A child who is adequately rested, consistently nourished, properly hydrated, and not fighting a physical burden he has not told you about is starting each day from the best possible biological position for managing the challenges ADHD creates. That position does not eliminate the ADHD, but it meaningfully changes how much room the ADHD has to make things harder.

Chapter 6:
Movement, Sports, and the ADHD Advantage

Exercise is the single best thing you can do for your brain in terms of mood, memory, and learning.

Your son comes home from soccer practice and for the next two hours he is a different child. Calmer. More present at dinner. Willing to sit down and work through his homework without the usual forty-five minutes of avoidance and circling. You have noticed this pattern before without fully understanding it, filed it away as a good day or as something particular about that coach or as luck. It is none of those things. It is neurology, and once you understand the mechanism behind it, you can stop waiting for it to happen randomly and start making it happen deliberately.

The relationship between physical movement and the ADHD brain is not a soft wellness claim. It is one of the most consistent and mechanistically specific findings in ADHD research. The question is not whether exercise helps, because that is settled. The question is how to use it strategically: which kinds of movement work best, how to find an activity your son will actually stick with, how to handle the emotional intensity that sports bring out, and how to position movement in the daily structure so that it does its best work at the moments when the ADHD brain most needs it.

Why Physical Activity Is Non-Negotiable for ADHD Boys

Most advice about exercise for children defaults to the general claim that physical activity is good for everyone, which is true but gives parents of ADHD children no specific reason to protect their son's movement time against everything else competing for it. The specific case for ADHD is substantially stronger than the general case, and understanding why it is specific changes how much weight you give it.

When a child with ADHD exercises aerobically, his brain releases dopamine, norepinephrine, and serotonin in quantities that are directly meaningful to how the ADHD brain functions. These are not incidental byproducts of physical exertion. They are the same neurotransmitters that stimulant and non-stimulant ADHD medications target, working through the same prefrontal circuits that regulate attention, impulse control, and emotional regulation. A twenty-minute run does not produce the same magnitude of effect as a therapeutic medication dose, and the effect does not last as long. But the mechanism is literally the same. The exercise is acting on the same system, through the same pathways, via a different delivery method.

The research bears this out specifically. A 2012 study by Matthew Pontifex and colleagues had children with ADHD complete twenty minutes of moderate-intensity walking before taking a standard cognitive attention test. The children who exercised beforehand performed significantly better than children who had spent the same twenty minutes sitting, and the improvement was specific to the ADHD group in ways that pointed toward the exercise compensating for something the ADHD brain was not providing on its own. Subsequent studies have replicated the pattern across different types of exercise, different age groups, and different ADHD presentations. The finding is consistent enough that researchers no longer ask whether exercise improves ADHD-related cognitive function. They are asking how much, how long, and when.

The broader research literature on exercise and ADHD has produced effect sizes for exercise on attention and cognitive control that compare favorably to non-pharmacological interventions like behavioral therapy, particularly in the short-term window immediately following the activity. What makes exercise distinctive as an intervention is that it is available every day, it does not require a therapist or a clinic, and its effects can be observed within the same afternoon by any parent who schedules it consistently. The barrier is not evidence. The barrier is the cultural undervaluation of movement as serious intervention rather than optional recreation.

Timing is one of the most practically important variables. The neurochemical effect of exercise peaks somewhere in the thirty-to-sixty-minute window after the activity ends and then gradually declines over the following two to three hours. This means that exercise positioned before a period of cognitive demand, before school if possible, or before homework in the afternoon, produces its benefit exactly when it is needed. Exercise in the late afternoon that is followed by dinner, screens, and bed uses the neurochemical window during a period of low demand.

The same activity moved to thirty minutes before homework produces a measurably different homework session.

The implication that many parents find counterintuitive is that movement is not a break from learning. It is a neurological precondition for it. A child with ADHD who is asked to sit and sustain focus without having moved is being asked to produce a neurochemical state from a stationary position that his brain generates readily in response to physical activity. Cutting movement time to make more time for homework is not a neutral trade. It removes one of the primary mechanisms by which the ADHD brain prepares itself for exactly the kind of sustained cognitive work that homework requires. The homework then takes longer, produces more conflict, and results in poorer retention than the same homework completed after movement. Most parents who discover this through direct observation find it obvious in retrospect. The two-hour window your son has been giving you after practice was always the evidence. You just needed the mechanism to make sense of it.

Finding the Right Sport or Activity for Your Son

Not all physical activity produces the same regulatory effect for every child with ADHD, and not all ADHD children thrive in organized sports. Some do well in team settings and find that the social structure and shared purpose of a team give them a focus and a belonging that other environments do not. Others find that the social complexity of a team, the interpersonal friction, the waiting time on the bench, the coordination required to communicate with teammates under pressure, adds enough cognitive and emotional load to undermine the regulatory benefit of the physical activity itself. The net effect in those cases can be neutral or even negative, and forcing a child through a sport that is not working for him because exercise is important is missing the point.

Individual sports and activities tend to work well for boys who are overwhelmed by team complexity. Swimming, martial arts, gymnastics, cycling, long-distance running, and climbing all involve high physical engagement, strong sensory feedback, and a tight loop between what the child does and what immediately happens as a result. In martial arts, for instance, the learning is constant, the feedback is immediate, the progression through belt levels gives a concrete external structure to long-term development, and the physical contact involved in sparring provides the sensory input that many ADHD boys are chronically seeking. In swimming, the immersive sensory environment of being in water, combined with the rhythmic, repetitive nature of the movement, produces a focused state in some ADHD children that is difficult to achieve in any other context.

High-stimulation sports with fast pace, frequent direction changes, and physical contact tend to work well for the hyperactive-impulsive end of the ADHD spectrum. The activity matches the sensory appetite of a nervous system that is constantly seeking more input, so rather than fighting the need for stimulation the sport channels it. Soccer, basketball, hockey, and wrestling often land in this category. Lower-intensity individual sports work better for some children for the opposite reason: the simplicity of the demand reduces external noise and allows the child to enter a genuinely focused state without competing stimulation. A boy who cannot sit still in a classroom for twenty minutes may discover that running gives him the most focused mental state he experiences all week.

What your son will actually do consistently matters more than what a research paper says is optimal for ADHD in the abstract. The most neurologically beneficial exercise is worthless if it requires thirty minutes of argument every session. A boy who voluntarily spends ninety minutes skateboarding, who chooses to bike to his friend's house instead of being driven, who spends an afternoon at a climbing gym without any parental initiative, is getting substantial neurological benefit from activities that may not look like organized exercise at all. Physical activity does not require a coach, a uniform, or a schedule to count. The movement counts. The form is secondary.

The practical corollary of this is that parents should avoid the trap of deciding that an activity your son has voluntarily sought out does not count as real exercise because it does not have a coach or a scoreboard. Skateboarding involves significant balance, coordination, and proprioceptive feedback. Rock climbing involves problem-solving, sustained attention to body positioning, and a physical challenge that provides immediate and unambiguous feedback. Cycling provides rhythmic aerobic movement that many ADHD children find regulating in the same way running does. Labeling these as "just playing" while insisting on organized team practices misses where the actual neurological benefit is happening for that particular child.

When a child resists most physical activity, it is usually worth exploring whether specific barriers are operating rather than a general dislike of movement. A history of humiliation in competitive settings, social anxiety in team environments, sensory discomfort with certain physical conditions, or the accumulated experience of being last picked and publicly compared to peers can create an association between exercise and failure that looks like avoidance from the outside and feels like self-protection from the inside. These barriers are real and specific, and they respond better to identification and direct conversation than to increased pressure to participate in the activities that triggered them.

How to Handle Competition, Losing, and Frustration on the Field

Sports create a specific set of conditions that are particularly activating for the ADHD emotional system: visible performance under observation, immediate feedback that includes failure and correction, interpersonal dynamics with teammates that shift in real time, and the concrete experience of losing to a competitor who can be seen. For a child who already experiences emotions at higher intensity and returns to baseline more slowly than his peers, a hard game or a difficult practice is not just a minor disappointment. It becomes a full dysregulation event that extends well past the final whistle and often into the car, the dinner table, and the evening.

The pattern has a predictable shape. A mistake during play triggers a visible emotional response that is disproportionate to the moment, which then makes the next few minutes worse because the child is now managing both the original frustration and the self-consciousness about the reaction. A correction from a coach lands as a public criticism, triggering rejection sensitivity and producing either explosive anger or sudden withdrawal. A loss generates an emotional response intense enough that a parent tries to talk the child through it on the drive home, which extends the activation rather than closing it. By the time they arrive, everyone is depleted and the sports experience itself is associated with distress.

The most important thing you can do in the acute period, immediately during or after a difficult moment, is not to problem-solve or teach. The prefrontal circuits that process rational input and convert it into behavioral learning are disrupted during the emotional flood. Your son is not withholding his capacity to reflect. It is genuinely unavailable to him while the regulation system is in the red. Talking at him during this period produces escalation and defensiveness, not insight. What the acute period requires from you is stability: a calm presence, minimum input, no new demands, and no expressions of disappointment that add to his existing distress. Physical space is often more useful than proximity. Silence is often more useful than reassurance.

The useful conversation, the one where something can actually be processed and retained, happens thirty minutes or more after he has returned to baseline, and it looks less like a debrief than like a low-pressure check-in. Not "let's talk about what happened with the coach." More like "that looked hard. What was going through your head right then?" If he engages, you can follow the thread without turning it into a lesson. If he deflects, let it go. The relationship between you and your son across these moments, whether he experiences you as someone who appears when things go wrong with advice and disappointment or as someone who is still there when the storm has passed without judgment, shapes whether he comes to you with the next hard thing.

Coaches are part of this landscape. Many coaches have no context for ADHD and interpret the behavioral expressions of it as attitude, lack of discipline, or disrespect. A brief, early-season conversation framed as providing context rather than requesting accommodation can change how a coach responds when difficult moments arise. Telling him that your son takes corrections very hard emotionally, that it is not defiance but sensitivity, and that a quiet one-on-one follow-up works better than a public correction in the moment gives the coach a specific behavioral alternative rather than just a diagnosis to file away. Most coaches, given this information early, are willing to make that adjustment. The ones who are not, who insist that your son needs to control himself better or that you are making excuses for him, are giving you information about the environment your son is practicing in every week. That information is worth acting on.

There is also a longer arc to track across the season. Boys with ADHD who accumulate significant negative experiences in sports, who come to associate physical competition with emotional failure and public embarrassment, sometimes withdraw from physical activity entirely in adolescence. They stop signing up, stop accepting invitations to play, and develop an identity that does not include the physical domain. This is a loss that compounds: the neurological benefit of exercise disappears, and the social belonging that sports can provide disappears with it. Catching the pattern early, before it calcifies, is part of what the emotional management work in this section is ultimately about.

Using Movement Breaks Strategically at Home

The neurological benefit of exercise does not require an organized sport or a full practice session. Brief periods of physical activity placed at the right moments in the day produce real regulatory effects, and the home is the environment where parents have the most direct control over when and how movement happens.

The placement that consistently produces the clearest effect is before cognitively demanding tasks rather than after them. A child who arrives home from school and sits down immediately to homework is starting that homework at the worst moment of his regulatory day. He has been suppressing impulses, managing social demands, following instructions, and regulating himself in a demanding institutional environment for seven hours. The decompression that happens when he walks in the door is physiological: the compressed regulatory system releasing tension it has been holding since morning. Asking him to immediately begin another period of sustained cognitive effort skips the decompression phase entirely and puts him into homework while his nervous system is still discharging.

A ten-minute physical activity before homework, with enough intensity to elevate the heart rate and involve the whole body, changes what follows. Jumping on a trampoline, shooting baskets, running around the block, doing pull-ups on a doorframe bar, the specific activity matters less than the physiological state it produces. After the movement, neurochemical levels have shifted, the accumulated regulatory tension has been partially discharged, and the homework period that follows is typically shorter, less conflictual, and more productive. Parents who try this experimentally almost always notice the difference immediately, and once noticed it becomes difficult to return to the prior arrangement.

The distinction between a regulatory break and a distraction is worth being explicit about, because the child will often prefer the distraction. A break that involves a screen, even a short one, does not produce the neurochemical reset that makes the next period of work more accessible. It may feel like relaxation to the child, but it maintains or increases central nervous system activation in a way that leaves the regulatory system in approximately the same state it was in before the break. A break that involves actual physical movement, body engagement, and elevated heart rate produces a measurably different state. The question when a child resists physical movement and requests screen time as a break is not whether to give a break, but what kind of break actually serves the goal.

Movement breaks during the homework session itself are also underused. A child who has been working for twenty minutes and is beginning to show signs of difficulty, increased restlessness, obvious loss of focus, low-level irritability that is starting to build, is providing early warning that the regulatory window is closing. A five-minute movement break inserted at that point, before the behavior escalates, resets the clock and often allows a productive second period to follow. Waiting for the behavior to deteriorate into a conflict before responding produces an already-activated child who is harder to re-engage and less productive in the period that follows. The break used preventively is far more efficient than the break used as a de-escalation tool after the fact.

One practical framework that some families find useful is designating specific anchored movement points in the daily structure rather than relying on judgment about when a break is needed. A movement anchor is a fixed point in the routine where physical activity happens regardless of how the child seems to be doing. Before homework is one. Between homework and dinner is another. Before the bedtime wind-down is a third. Having these points defined in advance removes the negotiation about whether a break is warranted, because the break is structural rather than earned. The child knows it is coming, which makes the period before it more tolerable, and the parent does not have to assess and decide in real time, which removes a significant source of daily friction.

What Happens in the Brain During Exercise

John Ratey, a Harvard psychiatrist who has spent decades studying the neuroscience of physical activity, describes BDNF, brain-derived neurotrophic factor, as "Miracle-Gro for the brain." The phrase is almost embarrassingly accurate. BDNF is a protein synthesized in the brain during and after aerobic exercise, and its primary function is to support the survival, growth, and differentiation of neurons, as well as the formation of new synaptic connections. It creates the biological conditions in which learning, in the most literal neurological sense of the word, becomes more efficient.

BDNF levels increase significantly during sustained aerobic exercise and remain elevated for a period after the activity ends. During this period, the brain is in a state of heightened neuroplasticity: more receptive to forming and consolidating new connections, more efficient at encoding new information, more capable of integrating learning across different domains. This is not a metaphor for cognitive openness. It is a specific protein-level biological state that can be measured, that responds predictably to aerobic exercise, and that has been linked in research studies to improvements in learning and memory outcomes. The implications for when a child does homework relative to when he exercises are direct and practical.

For the ADHD brain specifically, the BDNF benefit is layered on top of the catecholamine effects described in the first section of this chapter. Dopamine and norepinephrine act on the prefrontal circuits that regulate attention and impulse control, producing the immediate functional improvement in focus and emotional regulation that parents observe in the hours after their son exercises. BDNF operates on a somewhat different timeline and mechanism, supporting the structural conditions in which whatever learning happens during that window is more likely to be encoded and retained. The two effects together mean that exercise before a learning period does not just make the child more able to sit still and pay attention. It makes the brain more capable of actually learning what it encounters.

The practical argument this makes for parents is specific and strong. When the schedule is compressed, when there is a test the next day, when the homework load is heavy, movement is the thing that gets cut because it looks like the obvious trade: less time playing, more time working. The neuroscience reverses this logic. Removing movement to extend homework time is removing the preparation that makes the homework time productive. Your son will spend more time on the same work, retain less of it, and experience the homework period as more aversive, because the neurochemical and structural conditions that would have made it manageable were cut to make room for it. This is the trade that looks rational on a schedule and is counterproductive in practice.

Protecting your son's movement time, even when everything else is competing for it, is one of the most evidence-backed interventions available to you that requires no prescription, no appointment, and no cost beyond a commitment to the schedule. It does not replace medication for children who need it. It does not solve executive function deficits or remodel the ADHD brain in the ways that long-term treatment does. What it does, reliably and within hours, is move the ADHD brain toward its own best functional state through a mechanism that is always available, produces no side effects, and compounds in benefit across a consistent daily practice.

The serotonin component of the exercise effect deserves mention alongside the dopamine and norepinephrine discussion, because its contribution operates somewhat differently. Serotonin is involved primarily in mood regulation, anxiety modulation, and the general sense of well-being that creates the emotional baseline from which cognitive performance operates. Boys with ADHD who also experience significant anxiety or emotional dysregulation, which is common given the frequent overlap between ADHD and both conditions, often show particularly pronounced mood benefits from regular aerobic exercise. Over time and with consistent practice, regular exercisers in this population frequently show reductions in the frequency and intensity of dysregulation episodes that go beyond what the immediate post-exercise neurochemical window would predict. The accumulated daily return to a regulated baseline appears to build regulatory capacity incrementally rather than just providing a temporary boost. This is not a claim that exercise treats anxiety or mood disorders. It is a real and consistent secondary benefit that adds meaningful weight to the case for daily movement.

The consistency piece also matters more than parents typically expect. A child who exercises at moderate intensity for thirty minutes five days a week produces more cumulative neurological benefit than a child who does an intense workout once or twice a week. The regular, repeated exposure to the BDNF and catecholamine effects means the brain is regularly returning to its own best functional state rather than accessing it occasionally. Parents who build movement into the daily structure as a non-negotiable element, on the same level as meals and sleep rather than something that happens when there is time or when the child requests it, are giving their son a daily preparation that his brain uses. The compound effect of that consistency across months and years is not achieved by occasional intense exercise sessions that treat movement as an event rather than a daily condition.

Chapter 7:
Building a Home That Works for an ADHD Brain

Don't organize clutter. Eliminate it.

There is a question that many parents of children with ADHD eventually ask, usually quietly, often with some guilt attached to it: why can my son concentrate at his friend's house, or in a different classroom, or at the library, but not at home in his own room where everything is familiar and comfortable? The impulse is to read it as a motivation problem. He can do it when he wants to. He just does not want to at home.

The answer is usually more interesting and more actionable than that. Environments differ in ways that matter significantly to the ADHD brain, and those differences are not random. The friend's house may have fewer objects competing for attention in the room where they work. The library has predictable low-level sound rather than the irregular interruptions of a household. The different classroom may have fewer visual stimuli on the walls, or the seating may position him differently relative to sources of distraction. The ADHD brain is unusually sensitive to the structural qualities of its environment, which means the environment itself is a variable that can be worked with deliberately.

This chapter is about that leverage. Modifying the environment is often more effective and considerably less conflictual than trying to modify the behavior that the environment is producing, and most families find that the same child in a better-designed space performs better with less friction than the same child in a disorganized one. The changes do not require a renovation. They require a different way of looking at what the space is asking of the child who has to function in it.

Designing the Right Environment Before Changing Behavior

Behavioral economists and designers use the term choice architecture to describe the way that environments structure decisions without the person inside them being consciously aware of it. The layout of a cafeteria that puts fruit at eye level before the desserts increases fruit selection without anyone choosing differently. A library that faces desks toward a wall produces longer study sessions than one that faces them toward foot traffic. The environment is doing something to the behavior, and it is doing it invisibly.

For a child with ADHD, this effect is amplified. The ADHD brain is already working harder than average to maintain focus, suppress impulses, and hold a plan in working memory long enough to execute it. When the environment adds friction to this process, the additional cognitive load is real and it matters. A desk covered in objects that are not part of the current task means the child's attention is constantly being invited away. An open bedroom door means sounds from the rest of the house compete with the homework for attentional resources. A backpack that is never in the same place means the start of every homework session begins with a search, which is both practically disruptive and emotionally activating before the work has even begun.

The first principle of designing for an ADHD brain is to reduce the number of decisions the environment requires. Every decision draws on the same executive function resources that attention and impulse control depend on, and in a child with ADHD those resources are limited and inconsistent. When the environment makes decisions by default, such as when the homework spot is fixed and the materials are always there, or when the backpack has one location that is always its location, the child does not need to spend regulatory resources deciding where to start. The decision has already been made by the structure.

The second principle is to audit the workspace for competing stimuli. Sit where your son sits to do homework and look at what his eyes can fall on that has nothing to do with the work. Toys within reach. Open windows with movement outside. Posters or drawings on the wall in his direct line of sight. A television in the same room. Siblings passing through. Each of these is an attentional invitation, and a brain that struggles to hold focus will follow those invitations. Reducing the invitation count is not about punishment or deprivation. It is about removing obstacles that are getting in the way of a capacity the child actually has.

The third principle, and perhaps the most important one, is to treat the environment as a variable before treating the behavior as a problem. When a child is consistently struggling in a specific space or at a specific time, the first question worth asking is not what is wrong with him but what is the environment requiring of him that it could be making easier. This reframe is not permissive. It is practical. A child who cannot focus in a chaotic environment and can focus in a calm one is telling you something about the system, not about his character.

There is a useful mental exercise for any parent who doubts how much the environment is contributing to a struggle. Imagine asking your son to do his homework in the kitchen during dinner preparation: pots clattering, siblings talking, food smells, movement in all directions, no designated surface, materials scattered. Almost every parent can predict that would not go well. Now ask what the current homework environment looks like on the dimensions that matter most: visual stimulation, auditory interruption, available surface, proximity to distractions. The gap between the ideal and the current reality often contains most of the explanation for what is happening.

Reducing Visual Clutter and Sensory Overload

Many children with ADHD are more sensitive to sensory input than their neurotypical peers, and the home environment is often one of the most sensory-dense spaces they inhabit. Understanding which specific sensory channels are most activating for your son, and making targeted adjustments in the spaces where focus is required, is more effective than broad reorganization efforts that address everything at once and sustain nothing.

Visual clutter is the most commonly underestimated environmental variable. In a bedroom or workspace that is covered in objects, posters, collections, clothes on the floor, and open shelving full of visible items, the visual system is constantly processing background information that is not relevant to the current task. For a neurotypical child, this background processing is mostly handled automatically and does not significantly interfere with the foreground task. For a child with ADHD, the filtering between foreground and background is less reliable, which means that a cluttered visual field is genuinely more cognitively expensive to work in than a simple one. The question is not whether the clutter bothers him. He may not notice it at all consciously. The question is whether removing it changes what he can do in that space. The answer is usually yes.

Background noise is the second most impactful variable for most ADHD children, though its effect is not uniform. Some ADHD children are significantly disrupted by variable, unpredictable noise like household conversations, siblings, or television from another room, but are able to focus well with steady, predictable background sound such as white noise, brown noise, or instrumental music. The irregular sound is the problem because it competes for attention in a way that a steady, non-changing sound does not. If your son consistently does better work with headphones and a steady sound than in a quiet house with occasional interruptions, that is neurological information worth acting on rather than a quirk to work around.

Lighting is less commonly addressed but worth considering. Harsh overhead fluorescent lighting produces a quality of visual experience that is more activating and fatiguing for some children than warm, diffused lighting. If your son's homework desk is lit by a single overhead light that creates high contrast between the page and the shadows around it, replacing it with a desk lamp that provides even, warm-spectrum light over the work surface is a minor change with a potentially meaningful effect on sustained concentration.

The practical approach to identifying your son's specific sensory profile is observational before it is corrective. Notice where he settles voluntarily when he is trying to concentrate. Notice what he avoids. Notice whether he seeks out unusual positions such as lying on the floor, working under the desk, or covering his ears while reading. These are not random behaviors. They are a child attempting to regulate his own sensory input in the ways that his nervous system has found effective. What he is doing spontaneously often contains the answer to what the environment should be providing by design.

One common mistake is making all the changes at once and then attributing improvement or lack of improvement to the entire set of changes without knowing which ones were responsible. A more useful approach is making one change at a time, observing the effect over a week, and deciding whether it is worth keeping before making the next change. This slower approach produces a clearer picture of what is actually working for your son's specific sensory profile and builds a set of environmental adjustments that are grounded in observation rather than theory.

The adjustment process does not need to be sweeping to be effective. Removing the five most visually distracting elements from the homework area. Closing the door when the household is loud. Adding a white noise machine to his room. Moving the desk so it faces a wall rather than a window. Each of these is a single small change that can produce a measurable difference in the homework session that follows it. The goal is not a spare, silent room that no child would want to inhabit. It is a homework environment that asks less of the ADHD brain before the work even begins.

Visual Cues, Timers, and Tools That Replace Nagging

Every time a parent has to verbally remind a child with ADHD to do something he was already supposed to know he needed to do, two things happen. The child is reminded that he is failing to do something he should be doing independently, which is a small but real hit to self-concept repeated many times daily. And the parent is doing cognitive work that a system could do instead, which is a drain on the relationship over time. The question worth asking when a verbal reminder has to be issued is not how to make the child more responsive to it. It is how to design a system that makes the reminder unnecessary.

Visual cues work for ADHD brains where verbal reminders often fail for a specific neurological reason. Working memory, the system that holds information in mind between receiving it and acting on it, is less reliable in ADHD. A verbal instruction enters the working memory system, competes with everything else there, and fades. A visual cue at the point of action does not need to be held in working memory at all. The information is in the environment where the action needs to happen. It does not require retrieval. It only requires looking.

A laminated checklist on the bathroom door showing the morning routine in sequence, with pictures for younger children and text for older ones, replaces the five verbal reminders that would otherwise be issued between seven and seven-thirty. The child is not remembering the sequence. He is reading it each time, which means the working memory deficit is bypassed entirely. The same principle applies to a backpack checklist posted inside the front door, a homework routine posted at the desk, and a bedtime sequence on the bedroom wall. Each visual tool is a system that does not require the child to remember, does not require the parent to remind, and does not produce the friction that the reminder-and-non-compliance cycle generates.

Visual timers are worth their own emphasis. A timer that shows time remaining as a visual quantity, where the amount visible decreases as the time decreases, provides the external time information that the ADHD time-blindness deficit makes it unreliable for the child to generate internally. A child who cannot feel that twenty minutes is passing can see a red wedge shrinking. The Time Timer brand and similar products were designed specifically for this purpose. Positioned visibly in the homework area, they eliminate the need for the parent to announce "you have ten minutes left" and the child's resulting surprise that time is running out. The information is always current and always visible.

The transition from verbal reminding to visual systems is not always smooth. Children who are accustomed to parental reminders sometimes resist visual systems initially, partly because the reminder itself has become a form of interaction, and partly because using the system requires a level of independent initiation that the reminder was previously providing. He may tell you the list is stupid, walk past it without looking, or insist he already knows what he has to do. None of these responses means the system is wrong. They mean the transition is happening. The shift works best when it is introduced as a change for the parent's benefit as much as the child's: "I am going to try to remind you less, so let's make sure the list is good enough that you do not need me to." Framing it as a reduction in nagging rather than an additional task tends to produce less resistance.

Anchor points matter as much as the tools themselves. A visual cue that is not in the right location will not be seen. The morning routine checklist belongs in the bathroom, not on the kitchen counter where it was designed, because the bathroom is where the action happens. The backpack check belongs at the door. The homework checklist belongs at the desk. When you notice that a visual system is not working, the first thing to check is whether it is located where the relevant behavior needs to occur, not whether the child is choosing to ignore it.

Organized Spaces That Support Independent Functioning

The goal of organizing a child's space is not tidiness. Tidiness is an aesthetic value and it is largely irrelevant to function. The goal is independent functioning: designing the space so that the child can find what he needs, complete what he needs to complete, and transition between activities without requiring constant adult input to locate, initiate, or manage the process. A space that achieves this does not need to look like a magazine photograph. It needs to work.

The organizing principle that translates best to ADHD brains is visibility. Objects that are stored in drawers, in closed bins, or behind cabinet doors essentially do not exist for a child with ADHD. If it is not visible, it will not be used, and it will not be put away, because putting it away means placing it in a location that will make it invisible again. This is not laziness. It is a working memory and object permanence dynamic. Out of sight genuinely means out of mind in a way that is neurological rather than attitudinal.

Practical applications of this principle include open shelving with designated and labeled positions for specific categories of objects, hooks at the door for the backpack and jacket rather than a closet, a desktop organizer that keeps school supplies visible and accessible rather than in a pencil case inside a drawer, and a homework folder that lives in a specific visible location on the desk rather than inside the backpack. The system works not because it is elegant but because it reduces to zero the number of steps between needing something and having it, and between being done with something and returning it.

The desk setup deserves specific attention because it is where the most daily friction occurs. A desk that is covered in non-homework objects is not a homework desk. It is a storage surface that happens to also be where homework is supposed to happen. The transition from the surface's usual state to a homework-ready state requires clearing, which requires decisions about where to put things, which takes time and executive function and generates resistance. A desk that has only homework materials on it, with a designated place for each material that is always where it is, is ready for work the moment the child sits down. The difference in how homework sessions begin is significant.

A system that was imposed without his input will be resisted, and resistance is expressed as the system being ignored rather than rejected outright. A system that he helped design, where he had opinions about where things go and how they should be organized, carries his investment in making it work. This does not mean asking a child to design an organizational system from scratch, which is an executive function task that many ADHD children cannot do reliably. It means bringing a design to him, explaining the logic, and asking what he would change. The conversation itself builds understanding of why the system is structured the way it is, which increases the likelihood of following it.

The resistance that children with ADHD show toward organizational systems is often misread as oppositionality. It is more often a combination of executive function difficulty with the system's design and a history of being asked to maintain systems that were not actually compatible with how their brain works. A child who consistently cannot maintain a filing system for his papers is probably not refusing to maintain it. He is probably experiencing the number of steps between finishing with a paper and filing it correctly as too many for the available executive function at that moment. The solution is fewer steps, not more insistence. A single labeled tray on the desk that receives all papers, sorted once a week rather than immediately, is a system that most ADHD children can actually maintain.

Organization is also not a one-time project. Entropy operates on ADHD spaces at a faster rate than on neurotypical ones because the daily maintenance of returning things to their places is itself an executive function task that is less consistently available. Building a brief daily or weekly reset into the routine, a ten-minute tidy at a fixed time rather than an expectation of continuous maintenance, acknowledges this reality and creates a sustainable system rather than one that degrades quickly and is then abandoned.

Chapter 8:
The Morning and Evening Blueprint

Win the morning, win the day.

It is Monday morning. The alarm goes off at seven and your son does not move. You go in at seven-ten, remind him, and he says he is getting up. At seven-twenty he is still in bed. You go back in with more urgency. He gets up, wanders to the bathroom, loses track of what he is doing, and reappears in the kitchen at seven-forty without shoes or a backpack, asking what is for breakfast when there is nothing ready because breakfast was supposed to be his job. The backpack is somewhere. The homework from the weekend may or may not be in it. The car leaves in five minutes. Everyone is already in conflict before the front door has opened.

By the time your son walks into school, he has already spent forty minutes in a state of stress and friction. The teacher who sees him at eight-fifteen sees a child who is scattered and reactive, and the explanation for it left the house with him. This chapter does not explain why mornings are difficult with an ADHD child. Earlier chapters have already covered the neurological reasons: the executive activation that comes slowly after waking, the time blindness that makes urgency feel abstract, the circadian delay that means his brain is often still in low gear at seven in the morning. What this chapter does is show how to build a structure that reduces the damage systematically, without depending on motivation or spontaneous cooperation that is reliably not there on a Monday at seven.

The same logic applies to the evening. A structured evening routine is not a luxury. It is the preparation that makes the following morning possible, and the absence of it is often the real explanation for what looks like a morning problem.

Why Mornings Are So Hard for ADHD Families

The morning asks a child with ADHD to do the hardest possible things at the worst possible time. Every component of the morning sequence requires executive function: initiating a task without external prompting, transitioning between activities on a schedule, tracking multiple steps simultaneously, monitoring time while executing them, and managing the emotional friction that arises when any part of the sequence goes wrong. These are precisely the capacities that ADHD compromises, and they are all demanded simultaneously in the hour before school.

The timing makes it worse. For many children with ADHD, the circadian delay described in Chapter 5 means that the brain is genuinely not at its regulatory peak at seven in the morning. Executive systems are slow to come online after waking in any person, and in the ADHD brain this activation lag is longer. A child who will be capable of reasonable self-regulation by ten in the morning may be genuinely less capable of it at seven, not because he is choosing to be uncooperative but because the regulatory machinery has not yet fully engaged. Asking for full morning compliance from a brain that is still warming up produces the same result as asking a car to perform at highway speed before the engine has reached operating temperature.

Transitions are the specific mechanism through which mornings fail. The morning is a sequence of transitions: from sleep to waking, from waking to the bathroom, from the bathroom to getting dressed, from getting dressed to eating, from eating to gathering materials, from the house to the car. Each transition requires the brain to stop one activity, disengage from it, and initiate a new one. Each of those micro-steps draws on executive function. For a child with ADHD, each transition is a potential failure point, and with enough failure points in a sequence the whole sequence collapses.

There is also the sensory dimension of mornings that many parents overlook. Getting dressed involves tactile input that some ADHD children find genuinely aversive: tags in shirts, socks that bunch, fabrics with textures that produce discomfort. What looks like stalling over getting dressed is sometimes a child trying to manage sensory friction that the adults around him stopped noticing years ago. Addressing the sensory pieces directly, buying tagless shirts, the specific sock brand he tolerates, the waistband style that does not bother him, can remove an invisible source of morning resistance that had nothing to do with compliance.

The emotional fallout from a collapsed morning extends well beyond the morning itself. A child who has been in conflict with his parents for forty minutes, who arrived at school with visible evidence of the chaos on his person and in his bag, who may have been the proximate cause of the family being late, carries that history into the school day. His capacity for the kind of emotional regulation that a full school day requires is already depleted before the first class has started.

Understanding mornings as a compound regulatory event, rather than a collection of individual compliance failures, changes what solutions look like. The solution is structural, not motivational. No amount of reminding or consequence makes the executive system engage faster at seven in the morning. Removing the demand on the executive system does.

There is a useful reframe that helps parents approach the morning differently. Ask yourself what the morning would look like if your son simply could not do better at seven AM, if his executive system was genuinely running at sixty percent capacity and that was a fact of his neurology rather than a choice. What would you build around that constraint? That question leads directly to the structural changes that actually work, because they are designed for the brain that exists in the morning, not the brain that could theoretically cooperate if it tried harder.

A Step-by-Step Morning Routine That Reduces Conflict

The single most effective change most families can make to the morning is moving as much of it as possible to the night before. The night before, the regulatory system is less depleted, there is no time pressure, and decisions can be made with full cognitive resources. The morning, by contrast, is exactly the wrong time to be making decisions: the brain is not fully online, time is short, and every decision that has not been made in advance adds to the executive load of a system that is already at capacity.

Concretely, this means that by the end of the evening routine, the following should already be done: the backpack is packed and in its designated spot by the door, the homework is inside it, the clothes for tomorrow are laid out or hanging visibly in order, and breakfast is either prepared or the components are set out so that preparation requires no decisions. A child who wakes up to a backpack that is ready, clothes that are already chosen, and a breakfast that he only needs to eat rather than assemble is a child whose morning asks significantly less of the executive system. The gains from this alone, without any other change, are often dramatic.

The morning sequence itself should be fixed, short, and visual. Fixed means it does not vary: the same order every school day, without the question of what comes next ever being an open one. Short means the sequence contains only what is necessary and nothing else: wake, bathroom, dress, eat, shoes, backpack, out. Visual means the sequence is posted where the child is at each stage of it, not recited verbally by a parent. A laminated card on the bathroom mirror. A checklist by the breakfast table. The sequence is not something he should have to remember. It should be something he reads.

The wake-up time should be calculated backwards from the departure time with generous margins. Most ADHD families underestimate how long the morning takes and build routines that work only if everything goes perfectly. Everything will not go perfectly. Build in time for the shoe that is missing, the item in the backpack that needs to be found, the extra five minutes at breakfast. A routine that has slack in it is a routine that survives normal disruption. A routine that requires perfect execution fails on the first imperfect morning, which is usually the first morning it is tried.

Verbal reminders during the morning should be replaced with timers and visual prompts wherever possible. A visual timer set for the duration of breakfast tells the child when breakfast time ends without a parent having to announce it. A timer for getting dressed removes the "how much longer" negotiation. The parent's role in a well-designed morning is to ensure the structure is in place, not to manage each step of the execution. Over time, a morning that runs on visual systems and timers rather than parental instruction produces far less conflict, because the system is the authority rather than the person, and arguing with a timer is less satisfying than arguing with a parent.

One adjustment that parents often resist is the idea that they should have less active involvement in the morning, not more. The instinct when a child is struggling is to step in, manage, remind, redirect. In a well-designed morning routine, the parent's primary job has already been done the night before. The structure is set. The materials are ready. The visual sequence is posted. What is left is staying out of the way enough that the child can run the sequence rather than looking to the parent to be the sequence. A parent who fills the morning with verbal instructions prevents the child from practicing independence and ensures that the morning depends on the parent's active presence indefinitely. The goal is a morning that works even when you are distracted, late, or not in the room.

After-School Decompression and the Transition Window

The moment your son walks in the door after school is not the moment to talk about homework, the notes in his agenda, the thing his teacher said, or the plan for the afternoon. This is one of the most consistent findings in the practical experience of families living with ADHD, and one of the least followed pieces of advice, because the afternoon window feels urgent to parents who have been thinking about the homework all day.

Your son has spent six to eight hours in an environment that required him to sit still, follow instructions, suppress impulses, track multiple teachers' expectations, navigate social complexity, and regulate himself continuously. The self-regulation resources that make all of this possible are finite, and by the time he gets home they are largely depleted. What looks like the explosion at the door, the door slam, the irritability, the picking a fight with a sibling within the first ten minutes, is not aggression or defiance in the usual sense. It is a nervous system releasing the pressure it has been holding since morning. The container has been holding it all day and has now been set down.

Asking for homework or compliance or conversation during this window is asking the regulatory system to perform immediately after it has just finished a full shift. The request is not unreasonable from an adult perspective. From a neurological perspective it is asking for output from a depleted system and then interpreting the failure to produce it as unwillingness rather than incapacity.

What the transition window needs is approximately twenty to thirty minutes of genuinely unstructured time. Not screen time as a default, though that is what children often request, but time that is genuinely low-demand: a snack, physical movement, time outside, whatever the child gravitates toward that releases rather than adds stimulation. The snack is important on its own terms as well as in the context of the transition, for the blood glucose reasons covered in Chapter 5. A child who is also hungry on top of being regulatory depleted is harder to reach than a child who is only one of those things.

The transition window is not wasted time. It is the preparation for the functional period that follows. Families who fight through it to get to homework immediately rarely get better homework than families who allow the decompression and start homework thirty minutes later. They get more conflict, lower quality work, and a child who associates homework with the worst part of his afternoon. The thirty minutes is an investment in the two hours that follow it.

The transition into homework after the decompression window works better with a clear signal rather than a parental announcement. A timer that marks the end of unstructured time and the beginning of homework time functions the same way it does in the morning: it moves the authority from the person to the structure. "The timer went off" produces less negotiation than "I told you it was time." A brief ritual at the transition point, sitting down together to look at what homework exists before the child starts independently, serves two functions: it breaks the task into a known quantity rather than an uncertain one, and it gives the parent a moment to identify anything that needs unusual attention before the child is already stuck.

It is also worth acknowledging that some days the decompression window will need to be longer than thirty minutes, and that forcing the transition before the child is regulated enough to work produces homework that is neither efficient nor retained. A day with a particularly difficult social incident, a test that went badly, or a conflict with a teacher may produce a child who needs forty-five minutes or an hour before he is accessible. Reading the level of dysregulation accurately and adjusting accordingly is not permissiveness. It is efficiency: a child who starts homework regulated finishes it faster and with less conflict than a child who starts it while still managing an emotional residue from the school day.

Winding Down at Night Without a Fight

The evening routine is the morning routine's foundation. A morning that goes smoothly is almost always a morning that was prepared by a structured evening. An evening that runs late, ends in conflict, or does not include the preparation steps moved out of the morning will produce a morning that starts behind before the alarm has gone off.

The structural principle of the evening routine is the same as the morning: fixed sequence, visual support, minimum decisions. The specific content is different because the direction of travel is different. The morning routine ramps up toward engagement with the external world. The evening routine ramps down away from it. This means that the sequence of activities should move consistently toward lower stimulation, lower demand, and lower sensory input as the evening progresses. High-stimulation activities, physically active play, video games, emotionally intense interactions, should be earlier. Lower-stimulation activities, reading, drawing, quiet conversation, belong in the final hour.

The evening homework conflict is its own distinct problem that deserves a direct mention. Homework placed in the evening runs directly against the neurological timeline of many ADHD children on stimulant medication, whose medication effect has largely worn off by late afternoon and is functionally gone by evening. Homework attempted at eight at night by a child whose medication has cleared and whose regulatory reserves are already depleted will take longer, produce lower quality work, and generate significantly more conflict than the same homework done at four-thirty with an after-school snack and decompression buffer. Where possible, fighting to protect the after-school afternoon slot for homework is worth the effort. The evening slot is a poor substitute.

Device management in the evening is a practical source of significant conflict in most ADHD households, and the conflict usually comes from the same place: the transition off screens is abrupt and unannounced, the child is in the middle of something engaging that the interest-based nervous system is fully committed to, and the demand to stop produces the same kind of resistance as any other transition out of a high-interest state. The visual timer used elsewhere in the routine applies here as well. Setting a timer at the beginning of screen time that shows how long remains, rather than announcing a cutoff when the time has expired, gives the child the same information while it is still actionable rather than after the fact. The timer does not make the transition painless. It makes it predictable, and predictable is manageable.

The preparation steps for the morning, packing the backpack, laying out clothes, setting out breakfast materials, belong at a fixed point in the evening routine rather than being left to the end when the child is tired and the parent is done. Mid-evening, before the final wind-down, is the right position for them. By then the child has had enough decompression to be functional, and there is still enough time before bed that the prep does not feel rushed. Done consistently, it transforms what the next morning asks of everyone.

One final element of the evening routine that is often missing is a brief check-in that is not about logistics. Not homework, not the backpack, not tomorrow's schedule. A short, low-pressure conversation at the end of the day, a few minutes while sitting together before the sleep routine begins, about something the child found interesting or funny or worth mentioning, serves a function that the logistics of the evening cannot serve. It tells the child that the adult relationship is not entirely about compliance and management. In a day that has involved many corrections, many reminders, many moments of the parent managing the child's failures, a moment of genuine interest in what the child actually thought about something is disproportionately valuable. It does not need to be long. It needs to be real.

Chapter 9: Homework, Screens, and the Daily Battles

Children need the freedom to discover the world, not just to perform for it.

It is five in the afternoon. Your son is sitting at the kitchen table with a worksheet in front of him. He has been sitting there for twelve minutes. In those twelve minutes he has written his name, sharpened two pencils, asked for a snack, gotten the snack, and is now staring at the first question as if it were written in a foreign language. You are nearby, trying not to hover, watching the clock. The tension has a familiar texture. In three minutes, maybe five, something will happen that transforms this from homework to conflict. You have been here before. You know how it ends.

Then the screens. Your son's relationship with screens is the inverse of his relationship with homework: effortless engagement, immediate absorption, no coaxing required. You could remove the worksheet from in front of him and put a device there instead and the transformation would be instant. The contrast between those two states is not lost on him or on you, and it is the source of much of what makes this hour of the day the hardest in the family.

This chapter does not offer a solution that makes homework easy or screens simple to limit. It offers a framework for understanding what is actually happening in both cases, which is the precondition for finding approaches that reduce the conflict, even if they do not eliminate it.

Why Homework Becomes a War Zone and How to End the Fighting

Homework asks a child with ADHD to do the hardest possible things at the worst possible moment. By five in the afternoon, a child who has been in school since eight has spent seven hours managing the exact cognitive demands that ADHD compromises most: sustaining attention across subjects, following multi-step instructions from multiple teachers, suppressing impulses in a social environment, tracking assignments and transitions, and regulating himself in a setting that does not accommodate how his brain works. The regulatory system has been running at capacity or beyond since morning. It has very little left.

Into this depleted state, homework drops a demand that requires task initiation, self-monitoring, time management, and the emotional tolerance for frustration when the work is difficult or unclear. These are all executive function tasks. Executive function is the system most compromised by ADHD. The homework demand arrives precisely when that system is most depleted. This is not a coincidence of scheduling. It is the structure of the school day colliding with the neurological profile of the child it produced.

The concept that helps most here is cognitive load theory applied to task initiation. Every task has an initiation cost, separate from the difficulty of the task itself. For most children, this cost is low: they receive the instruction, form an intention, and begin. For a child with ADHD, the initiation cost is substantially higher, and it scales with the emotional valence of the task. A task that is low-interest, requires sustained effort, and carries the implicit threat of failure adds emotional weight to an already expensive initiation sequence. The worksheet is not just a worksheet. It is a demand that arrives at the end of a day that has already cost more than the child had.

The activation cost is the piece that parents most often misread. When your son stares at a worksheet for twelve minutes without writing anything, the most visible interpretation is that he is avoiding or refusing. The more accurate interpretation is that the task initiation system, the mechanism that converts knowing what to do into starting to do it, is not firing. The gap between "I know I need to do this" and "I am doing this" is exactly what ADHD compromises in executive function, and it is widest when the task is low-interest and the cognitive system is depleted. The staring is not defiance. It is a brain waiting for a start signal that is not arriving.

What reduces the activation cost is not more pressure from the parent. Pressure adds emotional activation to an already depleted system, which narrows the window of attention further and often triggers the emotional response that ends the homework session before it started. What reduces the activation cost is reducing the cognitive distance between the child and the first step of the task. This can mean sitting down with him to read the first question together and then stepping away. It can mean pointing to the specific line where the answer goes. It can mean asking him to tell you what he thinks the question is asking before he writes anything. Each of these provides a small push that the initiation system needs without doing the work for him.

Homework load is also worth raising directly, because in some cases the problem is not the child's ADHD but the volume and nature of the homework itself. Research on homework effectiveness, particularly for elementary school children, does not support the common assumption that more homework produces better outcomes. For a child with ADHD who is already at his regulatory limit by the time he gets home, two hours of homework is not two hours of learning. It is two hours of conflict and dysregulation that costs the family the evening and the child his recovery time. When the homework load is genuinely excessive relative to what your son can productively engage with, communicating this to the school in concrete terms, "he works effectively for forty minutes and then cannot produce anything useful," is a legitimate piece of advocacy rather than an excuse.

Structuring Homework Time for an ADHD Brain

Once the timing question has been resolved, which Chapter 8 covered, the question is what the homework session itself should look like structurally. The common default, sit down and work until it is finished, is designed for a child whose attention can be sustained across an extended period and whose ability to monitor his own progress is reliable. Neither of those is a good description of the ADHD brain, and the default produces sessions that run too long, deteriorate in quality, and end in exhaustion and conflict with little to show for it.

The most useful structural change is breaking homework into timed segments separated by short movement breaks. Research on cognitive performance and sustained attention in children suggests that working in segments of fifteen to twenty minutes with brief physical breaks produces better quality output over the same total time than working continuously. For a child with ADHD, the benefit is more pronounced. The break resets the neurochemical state, discharges some of the accumulated regulatory tension, and allows the child to return to the next segment with a slightly higher functional capacity than he left the previous one with. The break should be physical, not screen-based, for the reasons covered in Chapter 6.

The sequence question, whether to do the hardest assignment first or the easiest, does not have a universal answer. The argument for starting with the hardest is that cognitive resources are least depleted at the beginning of the session and the most demanding work benefits most from whatever capacity is available. The argument for starting with the easiest is that completing something generates momentum and a small dopamine hit that makes the next task more approachable than it would otherwise be. The practical answer is to watch your son and notice which approach produces better results for him specifically. Some ADHD children thrive on the early win of finishing something simple. Others stall indefinitely on easy work and need the harder task first before they have any sense of progress.

Your role during homework has a specific optimal position that is neither absent nor fully engaged. Absent means that when the initiation system fails to fire, there is no one to provide the small push that gets it started, and the session stalls before it begins. Fully engaged means that the parent is managing every step, answering every question, and effectively doing the homework alongside the child in a way that does not build the independent skills the homework is theoretically designed to practice. The position that works is nearby and available, responsive when asked, but not hovering or monitoring continuously. Physically in the same room or an adjacent one. Not sitting across from him watching him work. The distinction matters because the watched child often performs the activity of appearing to work rather than the work itself.

Age is a reliable guide for session length. For elementary school children, productive homework time typically runs twenty to thirty minutes before quality degrades noticeably. For middle school children, the window extends to forty or fifty minutes, though this varies significantly by individual. If the assigned homework routinely exceeds these windows for your son, the problem is not the structure of the homework session but the volume of homework being assigned, which is a separate conversation to have with the school.

One structural element that carries more weight than parents typically give it is knowing before the session starts what the homework is. Not knowing what the assignments are when the child sits down means the session begins with a retrieval task from a working memory system that is already unreliable, followed by a planning task, followed by the initiation of the first assignment. Each of these sub-steps costs activation resources before the homework itself has started. A brief check of the assignment notebook or school app at the beginning of the transition window, before the decompression period, means that when the child sits down for homework the work is already identified and sequenced.

Screens, Dopamine, and How to Set Limits That Work

The reason screens are so much more compelling to a child with ADHD than homework, reading, or most other activities available to him is not a character flaw or laziness. It is neurochemistry operating exactly as designed. Video games, social media, and streamed content are engineered to provide continuous dopamine stimulation through unpredictable rewards, immediate feedback, social signals, and novelty that refreshes constantly. For the ADHD brain, which is chronically underserved by the dopamine system in everyday activities, a screen environment that delivers dopamine reliably and continuously is not merely entertaining. It is neurologically satisfying in a way that few other readily available activities match.

This is why the contrast between your son in front of homework and your son in front of a screen is so stark, and why attempts to use screen time as a simple reward for homework completion often backfire. The gap between the neurochemical experience of the two activities is so large that the homework feels worse by comparison than it would have without the screen as the immediate alternative. A child who knows a game is waiting the moment the worksheet is done is not more motivated to finish the worksheet. He is more acutely aware of how little he wants to be doing the worksheet, because the alternative is vividly present.

What works for screen limits is predictability and advance notice. Not reactive removal. A limit that the child knows about in advance, a specific amount of time that begins at a specific point in the day and ends at a specific time, is a structure he can accommodate. A limit that is announced when the parent has decided he has had enough, or removed abruptly as punishment for something unrelated, produces the maximum possible resistance because it pulls a neurologically engaged brain away from peak absorption without warning. The child is not being irrational when he reacts intensely to an abrupt screen cutoff. He is responding to having something that was neurologically satisfying removed without warning or process.

The timer placed at the beginning of screen time, not announced as a warning when the time is up, is the same mechanism that works in the morning and evening routine. When the child starts screen time knowing that forty-five minutes is available and watching the timer count down, the end of screen time is predictable and visible throughout. The negotiation at the end is shorter because the child has been informed continuously. The cutoff is not a surprise. The transition is still difficult, because transitioning out of a high-interest state is always difficult for the ADHD brain. But difficult and predictable is substantially easier to manage than difficult and surprising.

The transition out of screen time also benefits from a brief warning before the timer ends. Even within a predictable structure, the final moment still lands abruptly without one. A two-minute verbal notice, or a secondary visual indicator that the time is almost up, gives the brain a small runway to begin disengaging from the high-interest state before the demand to stop arrives. This is the same principle as the transition warning before any high-interest activity, applied to the specific challenge of screen time endings. The goal is not to make the end of screen time comfortable, which it will not be. The goal is to make it predictable and minimally conflictual, which it can be.

The framing of screens as the enemy, as something to be rationed as punishment and minimized wherever possible, tends to make them more desirable rather than less. A child who experiences screens as a scarce and contested resource develops an urgency around them that a child with predictable, consistent access does not show to the same degree. Predictable limits are more effective than restrictive limits, because they allow the child to plan around the structure rather than perpetually negotiating against it.

When to Push and When to Step Back

One of the questions parents of children with ADHD ask most often, and find least guidance on, is how to decide in the moment whether to insist that the homework gets finished or to let it go for that evening. The answer depends on factors that vary night to night, and there is no rule that applies universally, which is why the question keeps coming back. What there is instead is a set of criteria that, applied consistently, produce better decisions than either always pushing or always relenting.

The first criterion is the child's current regulatory state. A child who is in the middle of a significant emotional dysregulation event is not producing usable homework regardless of how long you keep him at the table. The quality of work completed during emotional activation is lower, the experience is more aversive for both of you, and the cost to the relationship accumulates without a corresponding academic benefit. Pushing through active dysregulation does not teach persistence. It teaches the child that homework is associated with the worst emotional states of the day. The practical question is not whether the homework should eventually be done, but whether this particular moment is one in which doing it is actually possible.

A related consideration is the pattern over time. A single evening where homework does not get finished because your son was depleted tells you very little. A pattern of evenings where homework does not get finished because the combination of his regulatory state and the homework volume routinely exceeds what is manageable tells you something important. Documenting the pattern, including the time spent, the state of the child, and what was and was not completed, gives you the data to have a meaningful conversation with the teacher or school about whether the homework load is calibrated appropriately for a child with his profile.

The second criterion is the relative importance of the specific assignment. Not all homework carries the same consequence if undone. A worksheet that practices a concept the child already understands is a different situation from a project that represents twenty percent of the quarter grade or a reading assignment on which tomorrow's class discussion will depend. Calibrating the amount of effort and conflict invested in getting homework done to the actual importance of the specific homework is not capitulation. It is proportionality, and most families spend more conflict on low-stakes homework than the stakes warrant.

The third criterion is what would actually be produced if you pushed through. A child who is so dysregulated or depleted that the work coming out is wrong, incomplete, or barely legible is not benefiting from the exercise. Submitting that work produces no academic credit and reinforces to the child that he cannot do the task, even though the accurate explanation is that he could not do the task at that moment under those conditions. The distinction matters for how he understands himself as a learner.

There is also a fourth consideration that rarely gets named explicitly: what this homework session is costing the relationship. The parent-child relationship is the primary tool through which everything else in this book operates. A child who associates homework time with conflict, criticism, and escalating frustration is learning something about what it means to engage with school tasks, and what it means to spend time with the parent who is present during that experience. Neither lesson is the intended one. Preserving the relationship during the homework hours is not a secondary priority. It is a precondition for the rest of the parenting work to be effective.

Choosing to let a homework session end before everything is finished is not the same as accepting that homework will never be done. It means communicating briefly with the teacher about what happened, which is a different skill than the one most parents default to, which is hoping the teacher does not notice. A brief note that your son was not able to complete the assignment that night, with a sentence about what the barrier was, gives the teacher information and gives you a record of a pattern that may warrant a larger conversation.

Technology as a Tool, Not Just a Reward

The conversation about technology and ADHD children is almost entirely about restriction: how much screen time is too much, how to enforce limits, how to prevent gaming from taking over the day. This conversation is not wrong, but it is incomplete, because it treats technology as a source of problems to contain, not as a category of tools that can work for or against the ADHD brain depending on how they are used.

The ADHD brain genuinely benefits from certain categories of digital tools in ways that paper-based systems do not replicate. A digital calendar with reminders fires the notification at the moment the action is needed, bypassing the working memory requirement of remembering to check a paper planner. A task management app that breaks a project into visible, checkable steps provides the external scaffolding for a planning process that the ADHD brain cannot reliably run internally. A text-to-speech tool for reading-heavy assignments reduces the cognitive load for a child who struggles with sustained silent reading. None of these are accommodations that lower academic standards. They are cognitive prosthetics that compensate for a specific neurological deficit in the same way that glasses compensate for a visual one.

The distinction between passive and active technology use is the most practically useful frame for parents trying to navigate this. Passive use, consuming content that someone else has produced, scrolling, watching, reacting, is the category of screen use that produces the most dopamine at the lowest cognitive cost and the least learning. It is also the category of use that is hardest to stop and most likely to displace other activities. Active use, creating something, building in a game that requires planning, using a tool to accomplish a task, learning a skill through an interactive platform, involves the same neurological engagement as passive use but produces output and often genuine skill acquisition. These two categories should not be treated as equivalent for the purposes of screen time limits, because they are not equivalent in their effects.

The question of whether to allow devices during homework has a more nuanced answer than either "yes, because technology helps" or "no, because screens distract." The answer depends on what the device is being used for. A student who is looking up a definition, using text-to-speech to read a passage, or checking a digital task list is using the device as a functional tool. A student who is responding to notifications, checking social content, or has a browser tab open to something unrelated is using the device in a way that fragments the attention the homework requires. The practical solution is not a blanket policy on devices during homework but a set of clear rules about which apps are available during the homework window, enforced by parental controls if necessary, so that the device is a tool and not a source of competing engagement.

For specific tools, the most consistently useful category for ADHD children includes apps with visual timer functionality that run on devices they already use, task apps that support breaking projects into small sequential steps and checking them off, and text-to-speech or audio tools for reading-heavy content. The specific app matters less than whether the child actually uses it consistently, which in practice means finding the tool he will adopt rather than the tool that is theoretically best. Involving your son in the choice of tools, explaining what problem each tool is trying to solve, and allowing him to reject options that do not fit how he works produces more consistent adoption than selecting the tools for him based on reviews.

The goal is not to eliminate the recreational screen use your son genuinely enjoys. It is to make sure technology is not only working against him. A device that sits on the table during homework and fragments his attention is one version of that story. A device that reads the passage aloud when he cannot sustain silent reading, or breaks the project into steps he can actually track, is a different version. Both involve the same screen. The difference is how it is set up, and who decides.

Chapter 10: The Discipline That Actually Works

Children do well if they can. If they can't, we need to figure out why and help.

How many times have you applied a consequence that you already knew, as you were applying it, was not going to change anything? You took away the video games. You sent him to his room. You gave the same lecture you have given seven times before, watching his eyes glaze at roughly the same point in the third sentence. And the next day, or the next hour, the same behavior appeared again. The consequence had no effect that you could detect, and you were left with nothing to do but repeat it or escalate it, neither of which was working.

This is not a failure of parenting consistency. It is a failure of tool selection. The disciplinary tools that most parents use by default were designed with a particular model of child behavior in mind: a model in which the child knows what the right behavior is, chooses the wrong one, and can be redirected by attaching an unpleasant outcome to that choice. For a significant proportion of children, that model is accurate enough that the tools work reasonably well. For a child with ADHD, several of the assumptions in that model are simply wrong, and applying tools built on wrong assumptions produces the results you have been getting.

This chapter does not offer a discipline system that eliminates conflict. It offers a way to understand why the tools you have been using are not working and what to replace them with.

Why Traditional Consequences Backfire With ADHD Kids

The standard disciplinary consequence operates on a simple logic: behavior A produces consequence B, and after enough repetitions the child learns to avoid behavior A in order to avoid consequence B. This is operant conditioning, and it works reliably in laboratory settings and adequately in many real-world parenting situations. The precondition for it working is that the child can hold the connection between A and B in mind at the moment behavior A is about to occur, and that holding this connection in mind actually influences the decision.

Both of those preconditions are compromised in ADHD. Working memory, the cognitive system that holds information active in the mind while it is being used, is substantially weaker in children with ADHD than in neurotypical peers. The connection between last Tuesday's consequence and today's behavior requires that the memory of last Tuesday's consequence be retrievable and present in the child's mind at the moment the behavior is about to happen. For many ADHD children, it is not. Not because they are indifferent to consequences, but because the retrieval and application of that information in real time is exactly the kind of working memory task that the ADHD brain handles poorly.

The second problem is temporal distance. Consequences that arrive after a behavior are less effective for all children than consequences that arrive immediately during or just after the behavior. For ADHD children, this temporal sensitivity is dramatically amplified. A consequence delivered an hour after a behavior, or even fifteen minutes after, arrives into a brain that is no longer in the same state it was in when the behavior occurred. The emotional context, the environmental triggers, and the neurological conditions that produced the behavior are gone. The consequence is experienced as an event in the present, disconnected from the behavior it is supposed to be teaching about. The child is not being evasive when he says he does not remember why he is being punished. He is accurately describing a working memory system that does not archive the past in the way the consequence assumes.

There is also a third factor that is rarely discussed: the emotional activation that accompanies most disciplinary consequences makes the lesson harder to process, not easier. A child who is in a state of distress because a privilege has been removed, or because a parent is angry and disappointed, is in a state of heightened emotional arousal. The prefrontal cortex, which is responsible for learning from consequences and updating behavioral plans, functions worst under emotional arousal. The moment of the consequence, when the parent believes the child should be learning, is precisely the moment when the ADHD brain is least capable of the cognitive processing that learning from consequences requires. You are delivering the lesson when the classroom is on fire.

There is a version of this that parents sometimes observe clearly: the child who genuinely cries and apologizes after a behavior, who seems to fully understand what he did wrong and why it was a problem, and who repeats the same behavior within forty-eight hours. Parents often interpret this as dishonesty or manipulation. The more accurate interpretation is that the remorse and understanding that occurred immediately after the behavior happened in a specific neurological state, and that state did not transfer into the memory and behavioral regulation systems that would need to change for the future behavior to be different. He meant what he said when he said it. He was not lying. He was demonstrating exactly how the ADHD brain processes consequence and regret: fully in the moment, and incompletely across time.

None of this means consequences are useless. It means that consequences function differently for ADHD children, that they need to be immediate, specific, and low-intensity to have any effect, and that alone they cannot substitute for the proactive teaching approaches that this chapter describes.

The Difference Between Discipline and Punishment

The word discipline comes from the Latin disciplina, meaning instruction or training. Somewhere in its passage into everyday parenting language, it became synonymous with punishment, which is a response to past behavior. The distinction is not semantic. It points to a fundamentally different model of what the parent is trying to accomplish and how.

Punishment is backward-looking. It responds to something the child did and attaches a negative experience to it. The implicit theory is that the aversive experience will motivate the child to avoid the behavior in the future. As the previous section covered, for the ADHD brain this theory is unreliable because working memory and temporal connection, which ADHD compromises directly, are both prerequisites for it to function.

Discipline as instruction is forward-looking. It identifies what the child needs to do differently, understands why he is currently not doing it, and actively teaches the replacement. This shift sounds simple but has substantial practical implications. When a parent frames discipline as punishment, the question after a problem behavior is "what consequence do I impose?" When a parent frames discipline as instruction, the question becomes "what skill is missing here, why is it missing, and how do I teach it?"

The Collaborative Problem Solving model developed by Ross Greene, whose quote opens this chapter, is built on this frame. Greene's central claim is that children with behavioral problems are not choosing to behave badly but are lacking the skills to behave well in specific situations. The missing skills are typically executive function skills: flexibility, frustration tolerance, problem-solving. The appropriate response is to identify the specific situations where the skills break down, understand what the child's perspective on those situations is, and work with the child to find solutions that work for both parties.

For parents whose instinct has been to interpret behavioral problems as willful defiance, this reframe is both challenging and relieving. Challenging because it requires giving up the model in which the child is choosing to misbehave and the parent's job is to make that choice more costly. Relieving because it explains why the cost-raising approach has not been working, and offers a different lever to pull.

Ross Greene's model is structured around what he calls a Collaborative Problem Solving process. Before the next problem situation, when everyone is calm, the parent identifies the specific unsolved problem , not the general character issue, but the specific recurring scenario , and opens a conversation with the child that begins with curiosity rather than correction. "I've noticed that when it's time to stop gaming and come to dinner, things get really difficult. What's making that hard for you?" The child's perspective often reveals something the parent did not know. The transition is hard because he is always at a critical point in the game. The dinner transition feels abrupt. He does not feel the warning arrives with enough notice. These are solvable problems if they are understood as problems rather than as defiance.

What this looks like practically is naming the behavior gap specifically rather than the behavior globally. Not "you are irresponsible" but "you have trouble starting the homework without someone sitting with you." Not "you never control yourself" but "you hit your brother when you are frustrated and cannot find another way to express it." The specific version identifies a teachable target. The global version identifies a character flaw, which is neither accurate nor teachable.

There is a practical skill embedded in this reframe that takes time to develop: the ability to observe a behavior problem and identify what skill the child would need to have in order for the problem not to occur, rather than what punishment would make the problem stop. A child who erupts when the game is turned off needs a skill in transitioning from high-interest activities with sufficient regulation to manage the frustration. A child who cannot start homework without escalating into avoidance needs a skill in initiating low-interest tasks when cognitive resources are limited. A child who lies when confronted about a mistake needs a skill in tolerating accountability without shutting down. Each of these is a specific, trainable skill. None of them will be acquired through punishment, because punishment addresses the behavior after the fact rather than building the skill before the next situation arrives.

Natural Consequences Versus Imposed Consequences

Natural consequences are what happens in the world as a direct result of a behavior, without any additional action by the parent. The child does not put his shoes away and cannot find them in the morning. He forgets his lunch and is hungry at school. He is unkind to a friend and the friend does not want to play with him the next day. These consequences are immediate, logical, and self-administering. They do not require the parent to monitor, threaten, or enforce. They are also, for the ADHD brain, among the most effective teachers available precisely because they are direct and immediate.

Imposed consequences are what the parent adds: taking away privileges, assigning additional chores, restricting activities, time-out. These require the parent to be the agent of the consequence, which creates several problems. The parent becomes the aversive stimulus rather than the behavior. The child's attention is directed at the unfairness of the parent's response rather than the connection between his behavior and what followed from it. The enforcement burden falls on the parent continuously, which is exhausting and creates an adversarial dynamic that complicates every subsequent interaction.

The practical guidance is to allow natural consequences to operate wherever they are safe and the stakes are not too high. This requires tolerating the discomfort of watching your son experience the results of his choices without intervening to prevent them. For many parents this is genuinely hard, because the natural parenting instinct is to protect the child from negative experiences. In this context, that instinct works against the learning you are trying to support.

Natural consequences have limits. They do not work when the natural consequence is dangerous, when it falls on someone other than the child, or when the child has genuinely not understood what behavior produced what outcome. In those cases, an imposed consequence may be appropriate, but the most effective imposed consequences are those that are as close to natural as possible in their logic: losing screen time specifically because the screen was the object of conflict, not losing screen time as a general-purpose punishment for an unrelated behavior.

One category of parental response deserves attention because it is common and particularly ineffective with ADHD children: the delayed imposed consequence that has no logical connection to the original behavior. The child forgets his homework, so he loses his screen time. The child hits his brother, so he cannot go to a friend's birthday party two days later. The child is rude at dinner, so his allowance for the week is docked. Each of these is an attempt to apply something aversive to a behavior, but the aversive thing is disconnected in time and in logical relationship. For the ADHD brain, this produces the experience of the consequence as an event that is happening now for reasons that are not quite clear, which generates resentment and argument rather than learning. If you find yourself reaching for a consequence that is not connected to the behavior, that is a signal to stop and ask what the natural or logically connected consequence would be instead.

The principle that connects both types is immediacy and logical connection. A consequence that arrives immediately and follows logically from the behavior has a chance of reaching the ADHD brain.

One practical adjustment that helps parents implement natural consequences is shifting the language of explanation. Instead of "you're losing your device because of what you did," the language becomes "you left your bike outside and now it's wet. Let's figure out how to dry it off." The first framing positions the parent as the agent of consequence. The second positions the world as the agent of consequence and the parent as a partner in dealing with what happened. This small shift reduces the adversarial charge significantly and keeps the focus on what the child needs to do rather than on the parent-child power dynamic.

A consequence that arrives later and is logically disconnected from the behavior is, as the first section of this chapter established, unlikely to teach anything.

Strategies for De-escalating Meltdowns Before They Start

The most effective place to intervene in an escalating situation is before it becomes one. This sounds obvious and is consistently difficult to practice, because the signals that precede escalation are often easy to overlook until the window for intervention has closed.

Every child with ADHD has an escalation pattern. It has a characteristic sequence: a specific early signal that the regulatory system is getting stressed, a middle phase where the stress is visible but recovery is still possible, and a late phase where the behavior has become a full dysregulation event and nothing you do is helpful. Learning to read your son's early signal is one of the highest-leverage skills a parent can develop, because intervention at the early signal requires very little, while intervention at the late phase requires a great deal and often does not work.

Early signals vary by child but have a family resemblance: increased physical movement, a change in vocal tone or volume, irritability that seems disproportionate to the immediate trigger, withdrawal, or a particular quality of silence that is different from calm. Parents who have spent years with their ADHD child can usually identify these signals in retrospect. The goal is to recognize them in real time, when they are still actionable.

De-escalation at the early stage works through three primary mechanisms. The first is reducing the demand. When the regulatory system is under stress, adding cognitive or behavioral demands accelerates the escalation rather than interrupting it. This is not the moment for new instructions, corrections, or requests. Reducing what is being asked of the child gives the regulatory system space to recover rather than pushing it toward threshold.

The second mechanism is environment change. Moving from the location where the stress began to a different physical space resets the environmental triggers. The kitchen where the homework is happening, the living room where the sibling conflict started, the car where the argument about plans began , each of these spaces has become associated with the stress of the moment. Moving out of the space is not avoidance. It is a neurological reset that reduces the activation level.

The third mechanism is choice. Offering a genuine choice, even a small one, restores a sense of control to a child whose regulatory system is in part responding to a perceived loss of control. The choice does not need to be significant. "Do you want to take a five-minute break here or in your room?" gives the child agency at a moment when he feels he has none, which directly addresses one of the common triggers of escalation in children with ADHD.

The distinction between this section and Chapter 11, which covers managing full emotional explosions, is important. De-escalation strategies described here apply in the early phase, before the regulatory system has reached threshold. Once the behavior has become a full dysregulation event, the approach changes entirely: you are no longer de-escalating, you are waiting for the storm to pass. The window for proactive intervention is earlier and shorter than most parents assume, and missing it consistently means arriving always at the crisis rather than preventing it. The work of learning your son's escalation pattern is worth doing precisely because it extends that window.

Your tone is a variable in all three of these mechanisms. A parent who speaks in a calm, low, slow voice during early escalation is signaling safety. A parent whose voice rises, sharpens, or takes on urgency during early escalation is providing a cue that confirms to the child's nervous system that the situation is genuinely threatening. You do not need to feel calm to use a calm voice, but the voice matters more than the words you are saying.

One of the most consistent findings in research on parenting children with ADHD is that parental stress directly amplifies child dysregulation. This is not a criticism of parents; it is a description of a feedback loop that operates below the level of conscious intention. Your child's nervous system is reading your nervous system in real time, and a parent who is visibly stressed or frustrated provides neurological information that the situation is indeed dangerous or overwhelming, which accelerates rather than calms the escalation. The practical implication is that your own regulation is not separate from the de-escalation work. It is part of it. Finding a way to lower your own physiological arousal before attempting to intervene with your son is not a luxury. It is a prerequisite for the intervention to have a reasonable chance of working.

Consistency Without Rigidity

The advice most often given to parents of ADHD children about discipline is to be consistent. The advice is correct and insufficient. What it fails to address is the difference between consistency in what matters and rigidity in everything, and the practical impossibility of enforcing every rule every time for a family living with ADHD. Consistency in what matters means that certain expectations are stable, predictable, and reliably enforced. These are typically safety-related behaviors and the core structural elements of daily life: physical safety for all family members, the basic schedule of the day, the fundamental rules of the household. When these are consistent, the child with ADHD knows what to expect and what is non-negotiable. This predictability is itself calming and organizing for a brain that otherwise has to spend cognitive resources on what the rules are today. Rigidity in everything, attempting to enforce every rule every time with identical responses, is both exhausting and counterproductive. It is exhausting because the volume of rule violations in a household with an ADHD child exceeds what any parent can address consistently without becoming the household's full-time enforcement officer. It is counterproductive because it eliminates the parent's ability to make context-sensitive choices, which are often exactly what effective parenting requires. The practical framework is a clear hierarchy. Some rules are absolute and always enforced. Most expectations are consistent in their content but flexible in their implementation depending on the child's current state, the context, and what is actually achievable in the moment. This is not permissiveness. It is calibration.

The guilt that parents feel when they apply this framework, the sense that adjusting the expectation is giving in or sending the wrong message, is almost always misplaced. Your son is not learning that he can manipulate rules by appearing distressed. He is learning that the adults in his life are paying attention to him as a specific person, not running a rule engine. That is not a lesson in manipulation. It is a lesson in the kind of relationship in which change is possible.

The specific anxiety many parents carry is that adjusting expectations based on context will teach their ADHD child that performing distress is a reliable strategy for getting out of things. This concern is understandable but rarely borne out in practice. The child who learns that a dysregulated state gets him out of a demand is one whose dysregulation is being reinforced by that outcome, which is a real pattern to watch for. But the child who is genuinely dysregulated and receives an adjustment is not learning to fake dysregulation. He is learning that the relationship can flex when he needs it to, which is actually a precondition for him learning to come to the relationship when he needs help instead of escalating to force a response. The practical way to manage this concern is to distinguish between adjusting the demand and removing the demand entirely. Reducing how much homework gets done tonight because the child is genuinely depleted is different from eliminating homework as a category because the child finds it aversive. Shortening the time before screen access because the transition has gone unusually well is different from abandoning screen time limits because negotiating them is hard. The structure remains. The specific implementation adjusts. That distinction, held consistently, is what makes the approach coherent rather than permissive. The parent who holds firm on every rule equally, who never adjusts regardless of context, is often confused about what consistency means. Consistency means the same core values and non-negotiable expectations show up reliably. It does not mean identical behavioral responses to every situation. A parent who understands that difference is not inconsistent. They are reading their child, which is among the most sophisticated things a parent can do.

Chapter 11: Anger, Meltdowns, and Big Emotions

Between stimulus and response there is a space. In that space is our power to choose our response.

It starts with something small. A rule that is enforced the same way it has been enforced a hundred times. A no to something he wanted. A change to a plan he was counting on. And within thirty seconds, something that was a small friction has become a full explosion: shouting, crying, throwing things, slamming doors. The escalation was so fast you barely saw it coming. You are now standing in the middle of something that feels completely out of proportion to what started it, and you have two choices in front of you that both feel wrong: step in and risk making it worse, or step back and feel like you are abandoning a child who is drowning in his own emotional state.

This chapter covers the territory that Chapter 10 prepared the ground for but did not enter: what happens when the escalation has already completed, when the meltdown is in full force, and what comes after. The skills here are different from the preventive strategies in the previous chapter. They do not require catching anything before it starts. They require knowing what to do once you are already in the middle of it, and what to do when it is over.

Understanding the Emotional Flooding Cycle

The emotional flooding cycle has a structure, and understanding the structure is the most useful thing you can do for every other skill in this chapter. The cycle runs from trigger through escalation to peak, then through descent and into recovery. Every one of your son's meltdowns follows this arc, even when individual episodes look entirely different from the outside.

The trigger is the event that initiates the cycle. It is often disproportionately small relative to the intensity of what follows, which is the detail that confuses most people observing from the outside. The trigger does not cause the meltdown in the same way that a spark causes a fire in dry forest. The trigger initiates the cascade, but what determines the size of the response is the pre-existing state of the regulatory system, not the size of the trigger itself. A child who is well-rested, fed, and in a good regulatory state will absorb the same trigger that, on a depleted afternoon, produces a twenty-minute explosion. The trigger is the match. The regulatory state is the fuel load.

The escalation phase in children with ADHD is characteristically faster than in neurotypical peers. Where another child might have a minute or two of visible tension before reaching the emotional peak, an ADHD child may reach full flooding in fifteen to twenty seconds. This compressed timeline is not a character issue. It reflects the reduced inhibitory control that is one of the defining neurological features of ADHD, applied specifically to emotional regulation. The braking system is slow to engage relative to the speed of the emotional acceleration.

At the peak of the flooding cycle, the amygdala has taken over the processing of the experience. The prefrontal cortex, the region responsible for language, reasoning, consequence assessment, and perspective-taking, is effectively offline. This is not a metaphor. Neuroimaging research on emotional flooding shows measurable reduction in prefrontal activity and corresponding amygdala dominance during peak emotional arousal states. The practical implication is absolute: during the peak, there is no cognitive partner available for conversation, reasoning, or negotiation. The part of your son that understands cause and effect, that can hear your perspective, that responds to logic, is not present. Attempting to reason with a child at the peak of a flooding episode is not ineffective in the sense of something that does not work well. It is ineffective in the sense of something that is neurologically impossible at that moment.

The descent begins when the amygdala activation starts to subside. This does not happen because of anything you say. It happens because the neurochemical flood has a natural duration, and when the physiological arousal drops below a certain threshold, cortical function begins to return. The descent phase is often marked by crying that becomes quieter, physical tension that releases, or a shift from explosive to exhausted. The recovery phase that follows is a state of genuine depletion: the episode has cost energy, and the child is often more accessible but also more fragile than usual in the minutes and hours afterward.

There is a phenomenon that occurs in the recovery phase that shapes how parents typically respond. After a significant flooding episode, many children with ADHD appear remarkably fine, sometimes within minutes of the peak. They may ask to play, want a snack, or seem to have no memory of the intensity of what just happened. Parents often interpret this rapid apparent recovery as evidence that the episode was not genuine, that the child was performing, or that the emotional intensity was strategic. None of these interpretations are accurate. What you are seeing is the genuine neurological recovery phase. The physiological arousal has subsided quickly, because intense arousal states burn through their neurochemical fuel rapidly, and the regulatory system has returned to its baseline. The fact that the baseline is reached quickly does not mean the episode was not real. It means the descent from the peak was as fast as the ascent to it.

Understanding where your son is in this cycle at any given moment is the foundational skill for everything else in this chapter.

What Triggers Your Son and How to Map Them

Meltdowns feel sudden because the escalation is fast. They are not random. Every episode has an antecedent structure, and that structure repeats with enough consistency that it can be mapped and eventually anticipated.

Triggers organize into four broad categories. Situational triggers are environmental events: transitions between activities, changes to expected plans, waiting that extends beyond what the regulatory system can tolerate, and situations that require sustained compliance with a demand that conflicts with what the child wants to do. Transitions are the most consistent situational trigger across children with ADHD, because each transition requires initiating disengagement from a current state and engaging with a new one, and both of those are executive function tasks.

Relational triggers involve interpersonal experiences: being corrected, being criticized, being told no, feeling ignored or dismissed, perceiving a tone of disappointment or frustration from a parent or peer. Children with ADHD, many of whom carry a history of correction and criticism that is proportionally higher than that of neurotypical peers, often develop heightened sensitivity to relational cues that signal evaluation or disapproval. A parent who delivers a neutral instruction in a slightly flat tone may activate a relational trigger in a child whose nervous system has learned to scan for evaluative cues. The parent believes they said nothing loaded. The child processed something charged.

Sensory triggers are environmental inputs: loud or unpredictable noise, crowds, physical discomfort from clothing or temperature, sensory overload from multiple simultaneous inputs. Not all children with ADHD are sensory-sensitive, but many are, and for those who are, the sensory load accumulates across the day in ways that are invisible until the regulatory system is too full to absorb anything more.

Internal triggers are the body states that lower the threshold for all other triggers: hunger, insufficient sleep, illness, medication timing effects, and the accumulated regulatory fatigue of a long day. A child who would normally absorb a transition easily when well-rested and fed may not be able to absorb the same transition at four in the afternoon after a difficult school day with an inadequate lunch.

The practical tool for mapping your son's triggers is retrospective observation. After each significant episode, write down what was happening in the thirty to sixty minutes before the trigger appeared. Over time, patterns become visible. The episodes that seem to happen at the same time of day, in the same types of situations, with the same category of relational dynamic. The most useful format for this map is simple enough that you will actually maintain it: a note after each significant episode, written within an hour while the details are still present, that captures the time, what was happening in the hour before, the apparent trigger, and any internal state signals you noticed (was he hungry, tired, coming off a difficult day?). Over four to six weeks of this practice, patterns appear that are invisible from any single episode. You may discover that most of his hardest meltdowns occur on Tuesdays, which is his most academically demanding school day. You may find that transitions out of screen time produce explosions at a rate three times higher than any other trigger. You may notice that episodes cluster in the week before school breaks, when anticipatory excitement and schedule disruption combine to raise the baseline arousal level.

Once the pattern is visible, you have a different set of options. You can pre-load support on high-risk days. You can adjust the structure of transition moments that appear repeatedly in the data. You can communicate the pattern to your son in calm moments, not as a criticism but as shared information: "I've noticed that Tuesdays are usually harder for you. Let's think about what might help."

The map will not prevent every meltdown. It will allow you to anticipate and sometimes interrupt the conditions that make meltdowns likely.

In-the-Moment Strategies That Actually Calm Things Down

Once the flooding cycle has reached its peak, the intervention toolkit changes completely from what works in the early escalation phase. The strategies that are effective in the early phase, offering choices, changing the environment, reducing demands, are most useful before the amygdala has taken full control. At the peak, those same strategies may not be processable because they require the cognitive engagement of a prefrontal cortex that is currently offline.

The governing principle at the peak is input reduction. The ADHD brain at the peak of emotional flooding is overloaded with internal signal. Adding external signal, in the form of words, questions, explanations, or expressed emotion from the parent, increases the load on a system that is already at capacity. The most counterintuitive finding for most parents is that saying less is more effective than saying more, because saying more is experienced as additional input to be processed at a moment when processing capacity is zero.

Concretely, this means reducing your words to the minimum. Not a minimum that includes explaining your position, restating the rule, or expressing your frustration. An actual minimum: one or two words that signal presence without demand, or silence. "I'm here" said once, without elaboration. "I can see you're upset" said without a follow-up sentence. These are not conversation-starters. They are signals that communicate safety without adding cognitive load.

Physical space is a parallel tool. Many ADHD children at the peak of flooding need physical space as much as they need verbal quiet. Standing close, maintaining direct eye contact, or blocking the child's ability to move can all escalate the flooding by adding a layer of physical constraint to an emotional state that is already about containment and control. Moving to the periphery of the room, allowing the child to move, and reducing the intensity of direct engagement removes physical triggers without abandoning the child.

The parent's own physiological state is a direct variable in how the episode unfolds. Research consistently shows that children's nervous systems co-regulate with the nervous systems of the adults around them. A parent who is visibly tense, whose voice is elevated, or whose body language communicates urgency or anger provides neurological information that the situation is threatening, which sustains or deepens the child's flooding state. A parent who can lower their own arousal, slow their breath, and present a physically calm presence is doing something neurologically meaningful, not just modeling for the child but actively providing a co-regulatory signal that the threat has passed and it is safe to begin descending.

This is genuinely hard when your son is in the middle of a meltdown. Your own threat-response system is activated by the intensity of his behavior. Expecting yourself to feel calm is unrealistic. The goal is not to feel calm but to act calm for the specific purpose of providing the co-regulatory signal his nervous system needs. You do not need to suppress your emotional state. You need to manage its external expression during the episode, which is a different and achievable task.

One practical technique for managing your own arousal in the middle of an episode is the deliberate physiological reset: a slow exhale that is longer than the inhale, which activates the parasympathetic nervous system and measurably lowers heart rate within thirty to sixty seconds. You do not need to announce that you are doing this. You do not need to perform calm. You need to give your body the signal that the situation does not require emergency response, so that your external behavior can follow. Practiced regularly, this becomes a reliable tool rather than something you remember only when you are already fully activated.

A related practice is what to say to yourself during the episode, which parents rarely discuss but which significantly affects how they behave. The internal narrative of "this is unacceptable, he needs to stop right now" produces a physiological state that communicates urgency to the child. The internal narrative of "he is flooded, his prefrontal cortex is offline, this will pass in minutes if I stay calm" produces a different physiological state and a different behavioral response. The second narrative is also more accurate, which makes it easier to sustain.

After the Storm, Repairing and Reflecting Together

The period immediately following the peak is one of the most underutilized opportunities in parenting a child with ADHD. Most parents are still managing their own post-episode state: residual frustration, exhaustion, relief that it is over, or a mixture of all three. The child is often in a state of shame, confusion, and depletion. The temptation on both sides is to let the episode pass without processing it, because processing it feels like reopening something that has finally closed.

The post-episode window matters for the relationship more than almost any other single interaction. The child who exploded is not the child who is present now. The dysregulation has passed, the prefrontal cortex has returned to function, and the child who can think, feel, and connect is available in a way that was not possible during the peak. This is the version of your son who can hear you, who can experience reconnection, and who can take the first small steps toward understanding what happened.

The most effective opening is connection before content. Not a debrief, not a discussion of consequences, not a review of what he did wrong. A small physical reconnection: sitting near him, a brief touch on the shoulder if he accepts it, speaking his name in a tone that is warm rather than evaluative. The goal in the first few minutes after the peak is to communicate that the relationship is intact, that you are still on his side, and that what just happened does not define how you see him.

After the reconnection, naming what happened without judgment is the next step. "That was really hard" is different from "you lost control again." Both describe the same event but carry entirely different messages about who he is. The first names the experience. The second names a characteristic. Children with ADHD accumulate a significant weight of experiences in which their behavior is used to define them rather than to describe what happened in a specific moment. The naming-without-judgment practice is a small but consistent correction to that accumulation.

What not to do in the post-episode window is equally important. Delivering a lecture about the behavior while the child is still in the recovery phase is both ineffective and costly. The lecture tells the child nothing he does not already know, because the flooding itself was not caused by a lack of knowledge about the rules. It adds shame to an emotional state that is already depleted. And it signals to the child that the aftermath of a meltdown is primarily a punitive experience, which makes him less likely to come to you in the early stages of the next escalation when your help might actually prevent the peak. The window after the storm is too valuable to spend on the lesson that did not work the last six times.

The guilt that follows a meltdown for most children with ADHD is real and sometimes severe. After the flooding recedes, many children are genuinely distressed by what they did, what they said, or how they affected the people around them. This guilt does not need to be minimized, because minimizing it suggests that what happened was not significant. It also does not need to be amplified, because amplifying it increases the shame load without producing any learning. The most useful parental response to post-episode guilt is acknowledgment followed by forward motion: "Yes, that was hard for both of us. What can we do now?"

The repair process, over time, becomes itself a skill that the child internalizes. A child who has experienced dozens of post-episode reconnections learns that explosions do not end relationships, that the people who love him stay, and that there is a path back after the worst moments. This is not a small thing. Many adults with ADHD who had difficult childhoods describe not the meltdowns themselves as the most damaging experiences, but the aftermath: the withdrawal of warmth, the sustained disappointment, the sense that each explosion permanently altered how the parent saw them. The repair practice is the direct counter to that accumulation. It communicates, through repetition rather than through any single conversation, that the relationship is larger than any episode and durable enough to hold what just happened.

Teaching Your Son to Recognize His Own Warning Signs

Everything in this chapter so far has addressed what the parent does during and after a meltdown. This section addresses the longer-term project: helping your son develop his own capacity to recognize what is happening in him before it becomes something he cannot control.

This work cannot happen during or immediately after an episode. A child who is flooded or depleted does not have the cognitive resources for self-reflection on what he just experienced. The work happens in the calm windows: ordinary moments, maybe during a car ride or at the end of a quiet evening, when neither of you is activated and the distance from the last episode is enough to make it discussable without triggering the next one.

The conversation is about the body, not the behavior. Asking "why do you think you got so upset" is a cognitive-reflective question that most elementary and middle school children struggle to answer usefully. The question that works better is "what do you notice in your body when things start getting hard?" Most children, with time and a parent who asks consistently and without judgment, can identify physical signals: the tension in the shoulders, the feeling in the chest, the heat in the face, the quality of thinking that gets faster or louder or narrower. These are the early warning signals that the regulatory system is approaching its limit.

Naming these signals with a vocabulary that belongs to the child, not the therapist or the parent, is the first step. Once a child can name the signal, the next step is identifying one thing he can do when he notices it, before the escalation has gone further. Not a comprehensive self-regulation strategy. One thing. For some children it is moving to a different room. For others it is telling a parent they need a minute. For others it is a specific physical action that reliably reduces arousal. The thing matters less than the sequence: notice the signal, do the one thing.

The timeline for this work is long, and progress is not linear. A child who has learned to name his warning signals will sometimes still miss them. A child who can describe his escalation cycle in calm conversation will still sometimes be unable to access that knowledge when the escalation is actually happening. This is not evidence that the skill development is failing. It is evidence that knowledge and performance are different things, and that the gap between them closes slowly in ADHD, especially for emotional regulation skills that require the very executive function capacity that ADHD compromises most.

Parents who track this work over months, not episode by episode, will see genuine progress. The meltdowns become less frequent as the child accumulates more experience recognizing the early signals. The recovery time after episodes shortens as the child develops a more reliable sense of what helps him come down. The ability to use the one strategy he identified in calm conversation begins to transfer, imperfectly and inconsistently, into the actual moment. None of this happens on the timeline parents would choose, and none of it follows the smooth curve that would make it legible as progress from any given week's vantage point. It becomes visible looking backward over months.

This is not a short project. Self-regulation in children with ADHD develops later than in neurotypical peers, and develops at a pace that is slower and more irregular than parents typically expect. There will be meltdowns after your son has learned to name his warning signs. There will be meltdowns after he has correctly identified the early signals and still could not interrupt the cycle. Each of those is not a failure of the skill. It is evidence that the skill is still being built, which is accurate and expected. The work is to stay in the teaching relationship over months and years. Looking for evidence that the system has been installed and is now working reliably is the wrong frame. It is not installed. It is being constructed, slowly, through repetition and patience and every calm conversation you manage to have in between the hard ones.

Chapter 12: Connection Before Correction

Connection is the energy that exists between people when they feel seen, heard, and valued.

Think about last week. How many of your interactions with your son were about something he needed to do, something he had not done, something he had done wrong, or a transition that needed to happen? Now think about the interactions that had no agenda at all, that were simply the two of you in the same space doing something together or talking about something that neither of you needed to manage. For most parents of children with ADHD, the ratio has shifted over time in a way they did not intend. The relationship has gradually become predominantly corrective. Not because they are bad parents, but because a child with ADHD generates more correction-requiring situations than most parents anticipated, and the daily management load crowds out everything else.

This chapter is about what gets crowded out, and why protecting it is not a luxury but a functional prerequisite for the rest of the parenting work to be effective.

Why Your Relationship Is the Most Powerful Tool You Have

The first thing children learn to do with their emotions is not regulate them. It is co-regulate them with another person, specifically the person they are most attached to. Before a child can manage his own emotional state independently, he borrows the regulatory capacity of the caregiver. He uses the adult's nervous system as an external scaffold for his own, matching the other person's calm when the adult stays regulated, and amplifying when the adult escalates. This is not metaphor. It is the neurobiological process through which self-regulation develops, and it depends on the quality and availability of the attachment relationship.

For children with ADHD, this process is more protracted and more dependent on the external scaffold than for neurotypical children. The self-regulation skills that neurotypical children begin to internalize in early childhood are still being built, slowly and incompletely, in many ADHD children through middle school and into adolescence. The developmental window in which the child is borrowing the parent's regulatory system rather than running his own is longer. The quality of the attachment relationship, and the degree to which it provides a reliable, available, and warm base, matters more and for longer.

Research on attachment and executive function development points to a consistent finding: children with secure attachment relationships show better development of executive function skills over time than children with insecure or disrupted attachment, even controlling for baseline neurological differences. The relationship itself is a developmental variable, not just an emotional backdrop. This is particularly significant for children with ADHD, because executive function is the domain most directly compromised. A secure attachment relationship does not fix ADHD. But it provides the optimal environment for whatever executive function development is possible to occur, and it directly supports the co-regulation that the ADHD child needs during the years when self-regulation is not yet available.

A child who has come to experience his parent primarily as a source of correction and negative feedback develops a specific defensive posture toward that parent: he is less willing to disclose problems because disclosure leads to evaluation, less receptive to guidance because guidance comes embedded in a critical frame, and more likely to withdraw or react when the parent approaches because the approach has been associated predominantly with demands or consequences. None of this is conscious or strategic on the child's part. It is a learned adaptation to the relational environment. And it makes effective parenting significantly harder, because most of what effective parenting requires (the child's openness, cooperation, willingness to try suggestions, and tolerance for correction) is mediated by the relationship.

The practical implication is uncomfortable: the quality of the relationship affects the quality of everything else you are trying to do. The parenting strategies in every other chapter of this book are more effective when they are implemented in the context of a warm, connected relationship. They are less effective, sometimes significantly less effective, when they are implemented by a parent the child has come to experience as primarily a source of correction, control, and negative feedback. The correction still needs to happen. But connection is the condition under which correction lands, rather than the reward the child earns after he has improved his behavior.

Something parents of ADHD children rarely hear is this: the relationship has costs. The intensity of the daily management, the repeated conflict, the accumulated fatigue, and the grief of watching a child struggle produce real damage to the parent's own experience of the relationship. Many parents feel guilty about the ambivalence they feel toward a child they love deeply and find genuinely exhausting. The ambivalence is not a character failure. It is an honest response to an unusually demanding situation. Acknowledging it honestly, rather than suppressing it, is the first step toward the intentional repair that this chapter describes.

How to Talk to Your Son When He Shuts Down

One of the most consistent patterns in boys with ADHD is that direct conversation, especially conversation that involves conflict, evaluation, or emotional content, tends to produce shutdown. The face-to-face format of adult conversation, with its direct eye contact, evaluative framing, and expectation of verbal response, is precisely the format that creates maximum pressure on the processing systems that are most compromised in ADHD: working memory, verbal response under pressure, emotional regulation in an interpersonal context.

The first shift that helps is timing. Attempting to reach a child who has just shut down, who is in the immediate aftermath of a conflict, or who is still in the activation state that produced the shutdown is rarely productive. The window for connection is not when the parent feels the most urgency to reconnect, which is often immediately after the difficult moment. It is fifteen minutes to an hour later, when the neurological state that produced the shutdown has resolved and the child is accessible again. Waiting for the right window feels counterintuitive because the parent is still activated and wants resolution. But reaching into a shutdown state produces more shutdown.

The second shift is physical orientation. Boys, and ADHD boys in particular, consistently communicate more readily in side-by-side contexts than in face-to-face ones. A conversation that happens while driving, while building something together, while shooting baskets, while cooking, has a different quality from the same conversation attempted at a kitchen table with chairs turned toward each other. The side-by-side format reduces the evaluative charge, provides a shared focus that allows attention to oscillate between the task and the conversation, and does not require the sustained eye contact that many boys with ADHD find activating or uncomfortable. This is not a trick. It is an accommodation to the way the brain engages with interpersonal communication.

The parent who says "I noticed you seemed pretty down when you got home. I'm around if you want to talk" and then leaves the room is doing something specific: opening a door without standing in it. The child who knows the door is open and that walking through it will not result in immediate interrogation or a pivot to problem-solving is more likely to walk through it, in his own time, than the child who has learned that expressing distress leads directly to a parent who needs to fix something.

The third shift is lowering the demand for verbal response. Asking direct questions, especially questions that require the child to locate, formulate, and deliver a verbal answer on demand, is a high-executive-function task. Many ADHD boys who cannot answer "how was school today" as a direct question will talk at length about something that happened at school if the parent simply makes a comment about something related and waits. The presence without interrogation, the statement that opens a door without requiring the child to walk through it immediately, is often more effective than the question that demands a response.

One more shift is easy to miss: the parent's own emotional state during attempted connection. A parent who approaches a shut-down child while still carrying unresolved frustration from the triggering event communicates that state nonverbally, through tone, timing, and body tension. The child's nervous system reads that state before any words are processed. A parent who has had five minutes to lower their own activation before attempting to reconnect is physiologically different, and the approach lands differently. The wait is not passive. It is the preparation for effective connection.

A useful reframe for parents who have noticed their son shutting down consistently is to ask not "how do I get him to talk to me" but "what conditions make him most likely to talk?" The answer varies by child, but it almost always involves low external pressure, a shared activity or context, a parent who is not visibly waiting for a specific response, and a history of previous conversations where talking did not result in immediate correction or advice. That history is built slowly, through repeated low-pressure interactions, and it is the actual investment this section is describing.

Active Listening Techniques That Open Boys Up

Most parents believe they are listening to their children. In the sense of being physically present and taking in words, they usually are. In the sense of listening in a way that the child experiences as being heard, the gap between intention and execution is often larger than parents realize. The difference is not about effort. It is about specific behaviors that communicate to the child that what he is saying is being received without evaluation or interruption.

The most common failure mode in parent-child listening is the premature pivot to correction. The child says something about a problem, a frustration, or a conflict, and the parent, within two to three sentences, has moved from receiving the child's account to correcting it: pointing out what the child did wrong, explaining the other person's perspective, or offering a solution. From the parent's point of view, this is being helpful and efficient. From the child's point of view, the message is that his account did not receive its full hearing before the evaluation began. The child stops sharing because sharing leads, reliably and quickly, to being redirected.

The specific skill that counteracts this is staying in reception for longer than feels comfortable. When your son is describing a situation, a feeling, or a conflict, the goal for the first part of the conversation is to let him complete his account without adding anything to it beyond minimal acknowledgment. Not agreement, not disagreement, not advice. Acknowledgment: "I hear you," or "that sounds really hard," or "say more about that." Each of these signals that the account is being received and that there is space for more before the evaluation begins.

Validating the emotion before addressing the behavior is a specific sequence that helps enormously with ADHD children because it separates the two tasks that parents typically conflate. Validation sounds like: "That makes sense that you were frustrated. He kept changing the rules and that's genuinely annoying." It does not say the behavior that followed the frustration was acceptable. It says the frustration itself was understandable. This small distinction is significant because children with ADHD who feel their emotional experience has been dismissed or corrected before it was acknowledged often stop describing it, which means the parent loses access to the information that would help them understand what is actually happening.

Listening actively does not mean agreeing with everything the child says or refraining from having a perspective. It means sequencing: receive first, respond second, evaluate third. Children with ADHD who experience this sequence reliably from their parent show considerably more willingness to come to the parent with problems, which is the outcome that makes most of the rest of parenting more effective.

One specific pattern worth building intentionally is what might be called the open debrief: a brief, low-pressure moment at the end of the school day or before bed where the parent makes space for the child to share without the parent steering what gets shared. Not "tell me about your day," which is too broad and too demanding. Not "did anything hard happen today?", which assumes negative content. Something more like: "Anything from today you want to mention?" Said once, without follow-up pressure if the answer is nothing, and without a corrective response if the answer reveals something the parent would normally address. The debrief is listening practice, not a problem-solving session.

The failure mode to watch for is the debrief that turns into interrogation when the child discloses something concerning. A child who mentions that a friend was unkind today and hears the parent respond with a series of clarifying questions, suggestions, and proposed solutions learns that disclosure leads to a problem-solving session. He begins to calibrate what he shares against what he is willing to have processed aloud. The parent who can hear something concerning and respond only with "that sounds hard" and then wait has demonstrated something more valuable than any advice: that this is a space where he can say things and not immediately have them processed back at him. That demonstration, repeated enough times, is what makes the channel genuinely open. Its purpose is to keep the communication channel open rather than to extract information or address issues. Issues can be addressed later, when both parties are ready for that conversation.

Rebuilding Trust After Difficult Moments

Every parent who has spent extended time managing a child with ADHD has, at some point, lost their own regulation. Said something they wished they had not. Raised their voice beyond what the situation called for. Withdrawn in frustration or handled a moment with less patience than they would have chosen if the cumulative exhaustion had not been what it was. These moments happen. The question is not whether they occur but what happens after.

The emotional bank account is a concept that describes the accumulated balance of a relationship in terms of the deposits and withdrawals that daily interactions make. Positive interactions, moments of warmth, play, connection, successful collaboration, and repair make deposits. Negative interactions, conflict, repeated correction, expressed frustration, and moments of disconnection make withdrawals. The account does not need to stay positive at every moment. But the balance needs to be positive over time, because a relationship running on a chronic deficit has reduced capacity for the things that require the account to be in good standing: trust, openness, the child's willingness to come to the parent, and the parent's capacity to be effective as a corrective influence.

For parents who recognize that their balance has been running negative, the path back does not require dramatic gestures. It requires a sustained shift in the ratio of the interactions. More deposits, fewer unnecessary withdrawals. The specific content of the deposits matters less than their consistency and their genuine warmth. A parent who starts to notice and comment on things the child does well, who initiates small shared moments without an agenda, who repairs quickly after their own difficult moments, is changing the emotional context of the relationship in ways the child registers even when neither party is conscious of tracking it.

Parental repair is underused, and it is worth being direct about why. When a parent loses their regulation and handles a moment badly, the instinct is often either to ignore it and move on, or to offer a large apology that makes the child responsible for the parent's emotional state. The more effective approach is a brief, clear acknowledgment without drama: "I raised my voice in a way I shouldn't have. I was frustrated and I handled it badly. I'm sorry." Short, specific, and not requiring the child to respond with reassurance. This models the repair behavior that the parent is simultaneously trying to teach the child to use after his own difficult moments, and it demonstrates that the relationship is one in which accountability is practiced by everyone, not just the child.

One of the consistent findings in clinical work with families of ADHD children is that the parent's own mental health and self-regulation capacity directly affects the child's behavioral outcomes. A parent who is chronically depleted, who has no support, and who is managing the family alone carries a regulatory burden that eventually limits what they can offer. This is not a moral failing. It is a resource limitation. Parents who access their own support, whether through a partner, a therapist, a peer group of other ADHD parents, or simply structured time that is their own, maintain more capacity for the warmth and patience that the relationship requires. Taking care of your own nervous system is not in conflict with parenting your son well. It is a prerequisite for it.

A longer-term dynamic deserves attention: children with ADHD often sense the relational damage their behavior creates and carry real guilt about it. Many describe, as adults, a pervasive sense that they were too much, that they cost their family too much, that the parent who loved them was also worn down by them. This sense is corrosive to the child's self-concept in ways that persist into adulthood. The parent who rebuilds intentionally, who demonstrates through repeated deposits that the relationship is larger than the cost of managing the ADHD, is doing something that reaches beyond the daily management work. They are giving the child evidence against the narrative that he is the problem and the relationship is the casualty.

The Power of Play and Shared Time

There is research suggesting that twenty minutes of child-led play between a parent and child produces measurable changes in the child's behavior, cooperation, and emotional availability that persist across the following day. Twenty minutes. Not a vacation, not an elaborate planned activity, not an investment of resources the exhausted parent does not have. Twenty minutes of doing what the child chooses to do, without the parent steering, correcting, teaching, or managing.

The reason the child-led specification matters is that most of the time the child spends with his parent has an adult agenda embedded in it: there is something that needs to happen, something being taught, something being evaluated. Even positive shared time often has an implicit structure the parent is running. Child-led play is the specific format in which the child experiences the parent as a willing participant in his world rather than the manager of a set of demands the child is expected to meet. This experience is qualitatively different from co-presence, and children register the difference.

For exhausted parents, the barrier to play is often not time but energy. The cognitive and emotional load of managing a child with ADHD through a full day leaves many parents genuinely depleted by the evening, at exactly the point when the child is available for connection. The practical adjustment is to treat the twenty minutes as a deposit rather than an expense. Parents who try the practice consistently report that their own mood shifts during it, because play is itself a nervous system reset and the child's response to genuine engagement is typically more positive than the response to management. The deposit produces return.

What qualifies as child-led shared time varies by child and age: building something together, a board game the child picked, shooting baskets, cooking something he chose, playing a video game side-by-side where he is the one playing and you are genuinely watching. The unifying feature is that the agenda belongs to the child, the activity ends when the child is done rather than when the parent decides the time is sufficient, and the parent's attention is genuinely present rather than divided. The undivided attention is the actual mechanism. The activity is the container for it.

The behavioral rules during child-led time differ from normal parenting mode in ways that need to be stated explicitly and the transition requires intention. No instructions. No corrections. No teaching unless the child specifically asks. No phone. No steering toward a different activity. No commentary on how the child is doing the activity. These constraints are not about suppressing the parenting instinct. They are about creating a specific type of relational experience that is different from the rest of the day: a period in which the child is not being managed, not being evaluated, and not being redirected. The experience of this for children with ADHD, many of whom receive significantly more correction and direction than their neurotypical peers, is often visibly distinct. They are more relaxed. They engage more freely. They sometimes disclose things in these moments that they would not say in a direct conversation, because the low-pressure context has opened something.

Parents who practice this consistently describe a shift in the quality of the whole relationship, not just in the twenty-minute window. The deposits accumulate. The child who has regular experience of the parent as a playmate and a witness to his interests, rather than exclusively as a manager of his behavior, carries that experience into the difficult moments. The relationship can hold more because it has been built to hold more.

For parents who have not had a genuine no-agenda moment with their child in recent memory, the place to start is small: ten minutes, one activity the child picks, with the phone in another room. Not announced as "special time" or framed as a reward or a technique. Just the two of you, doing what he wants to do, with your full attention on it. The absence of agenda is itself the point. Your son does not need to know why you are doing it. He will know what it feels like, which is the part that matters.

Chapter 13: Social Skills, Friendship, and Belonging

Belonging is the innate human desire to be part of something larger than us.

There are moments in parenting a child with ADHD that are harder than the arguments, harder than the homework battles, harder than the school calls. One of them is watching your son try to connect with other children and seeing it not work. The invitation that does not come. The group that shifts away at recess. The comment he makes that lands wrong and he does not understand why. He comes home and says he does not have any friends, and the way he says it tells you he is not asking for advice. He is telling you about something that hurts.

The social difficulties that come with ADHD are not failures of caring. Children with ADHD almost universally want connection with peers. The problem is not motivation. It is a specific set of skills that most children acquire gradually and largely without explicit teaching, through thousands of small social interactions that provide feedback they can integrate. The ADHD brain processes social feedback differently, misses some of it, and sometimes cannot apply what it does register quickly enough in a live interaction. The result looks like social indifference or bad behavior from the outside. From the inside, it is usually something closer to confusion.

Why ADHD Makes Social Situations Harder for Boys

The social landscape of childhood runs on a set of implicit rules that are remarkably complex when you attempt to articulate them. You wait for the other person to finish speaking before you start. You calibrate how much you talk relative to how much the other person talks. You notice when someone's body language is saying something different from their words. You modulate your intensity in response to social feedback in real time. You read the group's temperature and adjust. None of these are rules that anyone teaches explicitly. Most neurotypical children absorb them through experience, integrate the feedback, and adjust their behavior accordingly across hundreds of interactions.

For a child with ADHD, several of the systems this process depends on are compromised. Working memory is needed to hold the current social context in mind while responding to it. Impulse control is needed to delay a verbal response until the other person has finished. Attention regulation is needed to track the other person's nonverbal signals while simultaneously generating one's own contribution to the conversation. Response inhibition is needed to calibrate the intensity of a response to match the social context rather than the internal emotional state. Each of these is an executive function skill, and each is directly compromised in ADHD.

The result in social interaction is a characteristic pattern. The ADHD child interrupts, not because he does not care about the other person's turn but because the impulse to speak arrives before the inhibitory signal that would normally hold it in check. He talks too much about his own interests, not because he is indifferent to the other child's interests but because the working memory required to track what the other child wants from the interaction is not running reliably. He reacts with an intensity that seems disproportionate to the situation, not because the emotional response is manufactured but because the regulation system that would normally calibrate the output is slower than the emotional activation itself.

Boys with ADHD also frequently miss or misread the social signals that would redirect their behavior. The moment when another child's body language is communicating "I'm done with this game" or "that joke went too far" is a moment that requires real-time reading of subtle cues, integration of that reading with an understanding of what it means in context, and a rapid behavioral adjustment. This sequence requires precisely the attentional and executive systems that ADHD taxes most. The ADHD boy often reaches the behavioral adjustment phase seconds or minutes after the window for it has passed, which means he experiences the social consequence without having had a clear subjective experience of making the error.

The way this plays out for boys has its own specificity. Boys' peer groups in elementary and middle school tend to operate through activity-based interaction, where the social currency is competence and participation in a shared activity rather than conversation and emotional disclosure. This format is in some ways better suited to ADHD, because the activity provides external structure. But it also introduces its own challenges: competitive games have rules, and rule-following under emotional pressure is exactly where ADHD shows up most visibly. A child who responds to losing with intensity that the group experiences as disproportionate, or who adjusts rules mid-game to accommodate his frustration, or who exits the game abruptly when things do not go his way, is engaging in behaviors that will affect his reputation in that peer group over time.

The history of these experiences accumulates. A child who has repeatedly had the experience of social interactions going wrong without understanding why develops a secondary layer of social anxiety and avoidance that compounds the original processing difficulty. By middle school, many ADHD children have learned that social situations are reliably uncomfortable and have begun to withdraw from them preemptively, which deprives them of the practice opportunities that might, over time, develop the skills.

Reading Social Cues and Understanding Unwritten Rules

The unwritten rules of social interaction are not intuitive for everyone. For neurotypical children, they are absorbed through a process that is largely automatic: the social environment provides feedback, the brain integrates it, and behavior adjusts. For children with ADHD, this automatic integration is unreliable. The feedback may not register in the moment it is delivered, or it may register but not connect to the relevant behavioral schema in time to affect the current interaction. The implication is practical: unwritten rules that most children learn implicitly may need to be taught explicitly to your son.

The teaching context matters as much as the content. Social rules explained in the immediate aftermath of a social failure are processed badly, because the child is typically in a state of shame, confusion, or defensive withdrawal. The prefrontal cortex that would need to integrate the lesson is not fully available. The lesson lands as criticism rather than instruction. The right context is a calm, low-stakes moment with no social failure in recent memory, where the conversation is framed as skill-building rather than problem-analysis.

Conversation turn-taking is one of the most teachable explicit rules. The visible cue that someone has finished speaking and is expecting a response is a combination of falling vocal tone, the person looking at the listener, and a natural pause. Naming these cues explicitly, and then practicing noticing them in low-stakes contexts, gives the child a concrete skill to apply. Some families practice this during mealtimes, with the explicit agreement that everyone waits for the three signals before speaking. The practice in a safe context builds the recognition skill before it is needed in a live peer interaction.

Intensity calibration is harder to teach because it is more context-dependent, but it can be approached through a shared vocabulary. The concept that different situations call for different levels of energy and voice, and that you can observe the other person's response as feedback on whether your level matches theirs, gives the child a practical frame. Some parents use a simple scale (one to five) that they develop together with their son, where they name situations that match each level. The scale then becomes a reference point: "this feels like a three situation" is more actionable than "calm down."

There is also a category of social rules specific to boys' peer culture that is particularly important to name: the rules around teasing and humor. Boys' friendships often operate through low-level teasing as a bonding mechanism, and reading whether teasing is affectionate or aggressive requires exactly the subtle social perception that ADHD compromises. A child who cannot reliably read the difference responds either by taking affectionate teasing as genuine hostility, or by extending aggressive teasing past the point where the other child finds it funny. Both responses create social problems. Practicing the distinction between playful and pointed, using real examples from the child's experience in calm moments, builds the perceptual skill the live interaction will demand.

Debriefing after positive social interactions, not just difficult ones, builds the child's conscious repertoire. When your son has a playdate that goes well, asking him what he thinks made it work develops his awareness of the social dynamics that he navigated successfully. This builds a repertoire of effective behaviors that the child can consciously access, compensating for the automatic social learning that the ADHD brain does less reliably.

The teaching sequence that tends to work best is: name the rule in a calm moment, practice it in a safe context, identify opportunities to apply it in real interactions, and debrief what happened afterward. This sequence is longer than the implicit social learning that neurotypical children do automatically, but it produces durable skill acquisition in a brain that needs the explicit pathway. Parents who go through this sequence consistently with two or three core social skills over a year see measurable change in how their son navigates social interactions. The change is not dramatic or uniform. It is the slow accumulation of a child who has more tools than he had before.

How to Help Without Hovering

The parent's instinct when a child struggles socially is to protect and manage: to arrange the right friendships, to coach the interactions in real time, to intervene when things go sideways, to buffer the child from social pain. These instincts come from a genuine place and are not wrong in moderation. They become counterproductive when they substitute the parent's social management for the child's own social experience, which is the only context in which genuine social skill development occurs.

The distinction between scaffolding and substitution is the practical line. Scaffolding looks like: choosing contexts for social interaction where your son is more likely to succeed (structured activities with clear roles, smaller groups, shared interest settings), briefing him before a social event with one or two specific things to try, and debriefing after with curiosity rather than correction. Substitution looks like: managing the other children's behavior, narrating what your son should do in real time during the interaction, intervening to resolve conflicts he could attempt to resolve himself, or selecting his friendships based on which children you think are appropriate.

Structured playdates for younger ADHD children are worth the planning they require. The unstructured "come over and play" format that works adequately for many neurotypical children can be overwhelming for an ADHD child, because it requires continuous self-directed activity selection and social negotiation without any external structure. A playdate organized around a specific activity (building something, a particular game, cooking together) provides a shared focus that reduces the moment-to-moment social demand. Shorter is also better than longer: one to two hours with a clear endpoint is more likely to end well than an open-ended afternoon that runs until someone is exhausted and dysregulated.

Group size matters more than most parents realize. Many ADHD children who struggle in groups of five or more are entirely functional in one-on-one interactions. The one-on-one format eliminates the need to track multiple social threads simultaneously, reduces the competition for speaking time, and removes the group dynamic management that requires the most executive function. If your son's social experience has been primarily in group settings where things go wrong, orchestrating one-on-one interactions and observing how they differ is diagnostically useful and often immediately more successful.

Identifying the context in which your son is most socially successful is one of the more useful things a parent can do. For many ADHD children, this is a shared interest context: a Lego club, a martial arts class, a coding group, a team sport with structured practice. Shared interest provides a ready-made connection point that does not require the child to manufacture social common ground from scratch. The ADHD child who seems to have no social skills at a general playground can be a completely different social actor in a context where everyone is talking about the thing he knows most about.

After a social interaction, a brief non-interrogative debrief helps calibrate the next one. Not "what went wrong" but "what did you notice about how that went?" and "was there anything you would do differently?" These questions, asked from a position of genuine curiosity rather than evaluation, invite the child to develop his own observational capacity, which outlasts any specific assessment you could deliver. The child who can observe his own social interactions is building a metacognitive skill that will serve him long after any specific advice has been forgotten.

One hovering behavior tends to go unrecognized precisely because it feels like attentiveness: narrating or coaching the interaction in real time during playdates. "Why don't you ask him what he wants to play?" or "Remember what we talked about taking turns?" delivered while the children are playing is experienced by the children as management, not support. It removes the child's ownership of the interaction and substitutes the parent's direction for the child's own social initiative. The playdate supervised this way provides social experience with training wheels that the child never learns to remove, because the parent is always there to correct the balance before the fall. The skill of managing a social interaction independently develops only when the child has the actual experience of managing it.

When Your Son Is Excluded or Bullied

Exclusion and bullying are experiences that most children with ADHD encounter at elevated rates compared to neurotypical peers, and they require a different parental response depending on the nature and pattern of what is happening.

The first distinction is between occasional exclusion, which most children experience at some point and which is part of the social landscape of childhood, and systematic exclusion, which is a repeated pattern in which the child is consistently left out by a specific group or in a specific context. Occasional exclusion hurts and deserves acknowledgment, but it does not require the same level of response. Systematic exclusion is a signal that something about the child's social experience in that environment is not working and needs to be addressed, either through skill development, environment change, or direct school intervention.

The parental emotional response to a child's social pain is often more intense than the child's own response, because the parent carries the weight of their own childhood memories, their fears about their son's long-term wellbeing, and the helplessness of not being able to fix something that matters. Managing this response separately from the conversation with the child is important because a parent who is more distressed than the child communicates that the situation is catastrophic, which amplifies the child's distress rather than containing it. Your son needs you to be a regulated presence who helps him navigate what happened, not a mirror that reflects the pain back at twice the intensity.

The conversation after an exclusion event should begin with listening and validation, following the sequence established in Chapter 12, before it moves to problem-solving. "That sounds really painful" before "here is what you should do next time." The child who is still processing the emotional hurt of being left out cannot access the problem-solving conversation until the emotional reality has been acknowledged. Many parents move to problem-solving too quickly because it is more comfortable than sitting with the child's pain.

There is a specific pattern that some ADHD children develop in response to repeated social rejection: they become provocative as a way of generating any social engagement, because provoking a reaction is more available than generating a positive connection. The child who pushes, teases past the acceptable limit, or makes disruptive comments in class is sometimes a child who has discovered that negative social engagement is more reliable than positive social engagement. Understanding this pattern changes the intervention: the child does not need more consequences for provocative behavior. He needs more access to positive social engagement, so that negative engagement is no longer the primary available option.

When bullying is the pattern, the school's involvement is appropriate and sometimes necessary. Documenting specific incidents with dates and descriptions, identifying the children involved, and requesting a meeting with the teacher or counselor gives the school the information it needs to act. Many parents delay this step out of concern that involving adults will make the social situation worse. In cases of sustained bullying, the cost of not involving the school almost always exceeds the cost of involving it.

One more dynamic worth naming: ADHD children are sometimes perceived by peers as odd or intense in ways that make them targets. They are also sometimes genuinely provocative in ways that blur the line between victim and contributor. Both things can be true simultaneously. A child can be treated more harshly than his behavior warrants and also contribute to the social dynamic that makes him a target. Effective advocacy with the school addresses both realities: what is being done to your son, and what supports he might need to reduce the behaviors that are contributing to the social difficulty. Holding both is harder than holding only one, but it produces more useful outcomes.

One element of the post-exclusion conversation that parents find difficult is resisting the instinct to promise resolution: "I'll talk to the teacher," "I'll call his mom," "I'll fix this." These promises, well-intentioned, shift the child's experience from "I have been helped to navigate something difficult" to "my parent will handle it for me." For older children especially, the sense of having someone advocate without taking over is more strengthening than having the parent become the agent of resolution. Sharing what you plan to do and why, asking the child what he thinks about that plan, and following up on what happened gives the child participation in the process rather than exclusion from it.

Building One Real Friendship Instead of Chasing Popularity

The popular understanding of what social success looks like in childhood is shaped by a norm that does not fit every child's profile. Popularity, defined as broad social acceptance and high status within a peer group, is a specific social outcome that depends on a constellation of skills, including social flexibility, broad interest range, and the ability to manage group dynamics, that are particularly challenging for children with ADHD. Chasing popularity for an ADHD child is often a path toward repeated failure and the accumulation of evidence that he is socially inadequate.

The reframe that helps most parents is shifting the target from popularity to genuine connection. One friendship that works is worth more than ten superficial acquaintanceships that do not. A child who has one person who understands him, who accepts his intensity, who wants to spend time with him for reasons that are real, has something that protects his self-concept and provides the social belonging experience that the research consistently identifies as important for wellbeing.

Finding that one friendship requires looking for a specific kind of match. The right friend for an ADHD child is not necessarily the most popular child in the class. It is the child who responds positively to your son's specific personality, who can tolerate and even enjoys his intensity, who shares at least one specific interest, and whose own social style is compatible with your son's. This may be another ADHD child. It may be a child who is also somewhat outside the mainstream social structure. It may be a child a year older or younger. The standard social categories that parents use to evaluate friendships (popular, well-behaved, the right crowd) are less predictive of success than the simple question of whether the two children actually enjoy each other's company when they are together.

Parents can actively look for the right match rather than waiting for it to emerge spontaneously. This means observing which children your son is drawn to, which children respond positively to him, and which of these overlapping sets share at least one specific interest. It means being willing to orchestrate initial contact (inviting the potential friend to a specific activity) and not waiting for the right friendship to assemble itself. Many ADHD children have lost friendships that were possible simply because the initial momentum needed to transform an acquaintance into a friend required a level of social initiative and follow-through that the ADHD child could not sustain alone.

Once the right match is identified, cultivating the friendship requires consistency over time. Regular contact, shared activities, and the parent's willingness to invest in facilitating the relationship (driving to activities, hosting at the house, maintaining the connection during school breaks) build the familiarity and history that deepen an acquaintanceship into a genuine friendship. One real friendship, maintained and deepened over time, provides more social protection than any number of social skills lessons.

The protective effect of a single genuine friendship for children with ADHD extends beyond the social experience itself. Research on children who struggle socially shows that having at least one reciprocal friendship buffers against the mental health consequences of broader peer rejection, including anxiety and depression. The child who knows that one person genuinely chooses his company has an internal social resource that changes how he experiences the rejection or indifference of the larger peer group. Parents who hold a broader social success metric for their ADHD child spend significant energy on an outcome that the child's neurological profile makes genuinely difficult. The energy redirected toward finding and cultivating one right friendship is more likely to produce something real. What does your son light up about? Who else in his environment lights up about the same thing? Starting there is not lowering the bar. It is finding the bar that is the right height for this child.

The one friendship is not a consolation prize. For many ADHD children, it is the most realistic and the most valuable social outcome available to them at this developmental stage, and the one worth protecting and cultivating with intention.

Chapter 14: School, Teachers, and Building the Right Team

It takes a village to raise a child. It takes a team to educate one.

You have been in this meeting before. Different classroom, sometimes a different school, but the same basic shape: a table with teachers on one side, you on the other, and a list of the same observations you have been hearing for years. He has trouble staying in his seat. He does not complete classwork. He calls out without raising his hand. He is easily distracted. He is not working to his potential. Every parent of a child with ADHD has a version of this meeting in their history, usually several. By the third or fourth year, the temptation is to stop expecting anything from it.

This chapter is not about hoping the school will eventually understand your son on its own. It is about building actively, deliberately, and strategically, the team that your son needs to succeed in school. Some of that team will be enthusiastic. Some of it will be neutral. Some of it will require management. All of it can be cultivated, and the cultivation is a parenting skill as important as anything else in this book.

What to Know Before Your First Meeting With the Teacher

The meeting with your son's teacher in September sets the tone for the entire school year, and most parents walk into it without preparation. They intend to explain their son, to advocate for him, and to establish a collaborative relationship. What often happens instead is that the conversation is shaped by the teacher's opening observations, the parent responds to those observations, and the meeting ends without a clear shared plan. The teacher has learned that this child has ADHD and needs some extra attention. The parent has learned what the teacher already knew. Neither party has committed to anything specific.

The strategic preparation for a first teacher meeting begins before the meeting with one decision: you are there to introduce your son as a complete person, not to present a problem. The teacher is about to spend six to eight hours a day with your child. The most useful thing you can provide is the information that makes it easier to reach him when he is struggling, harder to misread him when his behavior is confusing, and clearer what works for him when the standard approach does not. This is different from a list of diagnoses and accommodations. It is a portrait of a specific child.

Bring concrete observations, not complaints. Concrete observations sound like: "He does best when instructions are broken into steps and written down, rather than given all at once verbally." "He needs about five minutes of transition time between activities and does much better when he knows what is coming next." "When he is interested in a topic, his engagement is genuine and significant." Complaints sound like: "The last teacher never understood him" or "he always has problems in crowded environments." The first type gives the teacher actionable information. The second type creates a defensive dynamic before anything productive has begun.

The framework for the conversation itself should move in a specific sequence. Begin with what is going well (something genuine about your son's strengths, interests, or learning style that the teacher can actually use). Then describe the challenges in behaviorally specific terms, with the mechanisms behind them where you know them. Then propose specific collaboration: what you will do at home to support the teacher's work, and what you are asking the teacher to try at school. Close by establishing how you will communicate going forward: a brief weekly email, a communication notebook, a monthly check-in. The specificity of that commitment is what separates a productive first meeting from a conversation that does not change anything.

One practical tool worth bringing to the first meeting is a one-page summary of your son: his learning strengths, his ADHD-specific challenges, what works for him, what tends to make things harder, and one or two specific strategies that have helped in the past. Teachers meet twenty or more new students in September and receive minimal background on most of them. A parent who hands over a concise, well-written page of relevant information is giving the teacher a resource they can actually use. It does not replace the conversation. It supports it, and it remains on the teacher's desk as a reference after the meeting is over.

The first meeting is also the right moment to share what has worked in previous years and what has not. Concrete information from past teachers, from outside evaluations, and from your own observation of your son is genuinely useful to a teacher who is starting the year without any of it. You are not doing the teacher's job. You are giving them the information they need to do it better.

One conversation habit that helps in first meetings with teachers is resisting the impulse to apologize preemptively for your son. Parents of ADHD children often open with some form of "I know he can be a handful" or "I want to warn you that last year was difficult." These prefaces, well-intentioned, establish your son as a problem before the teacher has had the chance to form their own impression. A teacher who begins the year expecting difficulty tends to find it. The framing you use in the first conversation shapes the relational lens the teacher brings to the first week of school.

How to Build a Real Partnership With the School

A partnership with the school is built over time through patterns of interaction, not through individual meetings. The single best predictor of a productive school year for a child with ADHD is a parent who maintains regular, brief, constructive contact with the teaching team rather than disappearing for months and then appearing in crisis mode.

The distinction between productive involvement and counterproductive involvement is important to make explicit. Productive involvement means regular low-stakes communication, information sharing, acknowledgment of what is going well, and collaborative problem-solving when issues arise. Counterproductive involvement means frequent urgent contact, repeated complaints about the same issues without proposed solutions, communicating primarily when things go wrong, and escalating to administrators before attempting to resolve issues with the teacher directly.

Teachers have their own professional reality: they manage twenty to thirty students with varying needs, limited resources, and administrative demands that compete with their instructional time. A parent who makes the teacher's job easier (by providing useful information, following through on home commitments, and communicating in ways that are direct and proportionate) is a parent the teacher will go out of their way to support. A parent who generates anxiety every time they contact the school is a parent the teacher will manage rather than partner with. The difference in the child's experience of the school year between these two scenarios is substantial.

In middle school and beyond, when your son has multiple teachers, the communication challenge multiplies. You cannot maintain individual relationships with five or six teachers simultaneously at the level you could with one elementary school teacher. The solution is a tiered approach: identify one or two key contacts, typically the homeroom teacher, an advisor, or the teacher in the most challenging subject, and maintain closer communication with them while keeping other communications more targeted and less frequent. A brief, well-written email at the beginning of a difficult unit is more effective than a general complaint about a teacher's approach delivered at the end of the semester.

Managing the emotional content of the school partnership is a separate skill from managing its practical mechanics. Parents whose own school experience was difficult, who have accumulated years of frustrating meetings, or who have watched their son struggle while feeling unsupported by the institution can carry a reactive stance into communications that the current year's teacher did not cause and cannot reasonably address. Recognizing when your response to a teacher is being shaped by accumulated frustration from previous years is part of managing the partnership effectively. The teacher in September has not yet done anything to earn your distrust, and approaching them as if they have makes collaboration significantly harder from the start.

There is also a dynamic that some parents fall into after years of difficult school experiences: pre-emptively managing the teacher's impression of them by being very visible, very involved, and very present in a way that tips from partnership into pressure. Volunteering for every classroom activity, emailing multiple times a week without specific cause, or attending every school event with the explicit goal of relationship-building can signal anxiety rather than investment. The teacher who feels monitored is not more helpful than the teacher who is trusted to do their job. Regular, purposeful contact is effective. Pervasive contact is not.

The partnership works best when it runs on a predictable cadence that both parties have agreed to. Establishing this cadence at the first meeting, "I'll send a brief update at the end of each week, and I'd appreciate hearing from you if something significant comes up" gives the teacher a clear expectation and gives you a consistent touchpoint. A relationship with a defined structure requires less energy to maintain than one where contact is reactive and therefore always associated with something going wrong.

Documenting the partnership matters more than many parents realize. Keeping a brief record of communications, agreements made, and outcomes observed gives you a baseline for understanding what is working, a reference when there is disagreement about what was agreed, and evidence if you ever need to escalate. It does not need to be elaborate. A simple running note with dates and one-sentence summaries is sufficient.

Classroom Accommodations That Make a Real Difference

Accommodations for ADHD in the classroom exist on a spectrum from informal adjustments a teacher can make unilaterally to formal provisions that require a documented educational plan. Understanding the difference, and where to aim, is practical knowledge that changes how you advocate.

Informal accommodations are changes an individual teacher can make without any formal process. They require only teacher willingness and awareness. The most effective informal accommodations for ADHD are: seating near the teacher and away from high-distraction areas (doors, windows, talkative peers); instructions provided both verbally and in written form, either on the board or in a printed format; tasks broken into smaller steps with explicit checkpoints rather than assigned as a single long-horizon deliverable; immediate, specific feedback rather than end-of-period or end-of-week feedback; authorized movement breaks that are brief, non-disruptive, and agreed upon in advance. Each of these reduces a specific executive function demand that ADHD makes harder.

The critical reframe for teachers who are uncertain about accommodations is that accommodations remove barriers rather than lower standards. A child who cannot track multi-step verbal instructions and who receives them in written form is being given the same information as every other child, just in a format he can actually use. A child who takes a two-minute movement break before returning to a task is not receiving less instruction than his classmates. He is receiving the conditions he needs to absorb instruction at all. The accommodation does not change what is expected. It changes what the child's nervous system needs in order to meet the expectation.

Formal accommodations, such as those documented in a Section 504 plan in the United States or equivalent plans in other educational systems, carry legal weight and apply across all teachers. They are appropriate when informal accommodations have been insufficient or inconsistently applied, when the child's difficulties are significant enough to require written documentation, or when a change of teachers or schools would otherwise require starting the negotiation from scratch. Getting a formal plan in place during elementary school creates a documented record that follows the child and does not require re-establishing accommodations with every new teacher.

Extended time on assessments is one of the accommodations most parents of ADHD children pursue through formal channels, and precision about why it is appropriate matters. ADHD compromises processing speed and the ability to sustain attention under the pressure of a timed format, independently of the child's knowledge of the material being assessed. A child who understands the content but cannot access it under standard time conditions is not receiving a reliable measurement of his knowledge with a standard-time assessment. Extended time does not inflate the score. It removes the confound of processing speed from the measurement of content knowledge.

One accommodation that is among the most impactful and least discussed is reduced homework load calibrated to the child's productive working capacity. A child who is at his regulatory limit by the end of the school day and who is assigned two hours of homework will produce low-quality work through two hours of conflict. Advocating for homework that is calibrated to what the child can productively do, and having that calibration documented, addresses one of the most consistent daily points of family stress.

The conversation about accommodations with individual teachers is more effective when framed in terms of specific classroom impact rather than general ADHD characteristics. "He processes verbal instructions more slowly and tends to miss the last step when a multi-step task is given orally. Could you write the steps on the board?" is more actionable than "he has ADHD and needs accommodations for executive function." The first tells the teacher exactly what to do. The second tells them a diagnosis. Teachers who receive specific, implementable requests are more likely to act on them than teachers who receive general statements about a child's disability.

When the Teacher Is Part of the Problem

Not every teacher will understand your son, and some will actively make his school experience harder. This is a reality that parents of ADHD children encounter more often than parents of neurotypical children, because ADHD behavior is more likely to be misread as deliberate disruption, laziness, or disrespect. The teacher who believes that ADHD is an excuse rather than a neurological reality, who responds to dysregulation with punitive escalation, or who communicates to the child a persistent sense of disappointment will cause harm over the course of a school year. Knowing how to respond to this situation is a practical necessity.

The first step is documentation, before any conversation. When specific incidents occur (an email from the teacher that attributes your son's behavior to attitude rather than disability, a pattern of disproportionate disciplinary responses, a comment to your son that you believe is damaging) write it down with date, context, and what was said or observed. Documentation is not evidence of distrust. It is the record that makes any subsequent conversation specific rather than impressionistic.

The escalation sequence matters. The first conversation is with the teacher directly, conducted with the assumption of good faith and framed around the specific impact on your son rather than the teacher's character or intentions. "I noticed that when he is asked to move his card or change his color in front of the class, his anxiety for the rest of the day is significantly elevated" is a different conversation than "your behavior management system is inappropriate for children with ADHD." The first invites problem-solving. The second triggers defensiveness.

If the direct conversation does not produce change, the next step is the school's ADHD liaison, counselor, or special education coordinator, not the principal. Involving the principal before exhausting less confrontational options signals that you are not interested in collaboration, which makes every subsequent interaction harder. Moving gradually up the escalation ladder preserves the possibility of resolution at each level and demonstrates that you are a reasonable partner who has tried.

There is one scenario that requires a faster response than the gradual escalation sequence: when a teacher's approach is producing visible, significant harm to your son's self-concept or mental health. A child who is being publicly humiliated, who is told by a teacher that his behavior is a choice and he simply needs to try harder, or who is developing school refusal in association with a specific class does not need a months-long advocacy process. In these cases, involving the counselor or school administrator sooner is appropriate, with documentation of specific incidents. The timeline for escalation should match the severity of the impact on the child, not the parent's tolerance for conflict.

Throughout all of this, protecting your son's experience of the classroom is the operational priority. The child who knows that his parent is unhappy with his teacher develops loyalty conflict and anxiety that compound the existing difficulties. Your son needs to understand that adults sometimes see things differently, that you are working to improve the situation, and that his job in the classroom is to focus on learning while you work on the rest.

When the situation with a specific teacher is genuinely harmful and cannot be resolved through the standard escalation process, requesting a classroom change is a legitimate option. It should not be the first move, but it is not a last resort to be avoided at all costs either. A child who spends eight months in a classroom with a teacher who consistently misreads and penalizes his ADHD behavior is accumulating damage to his self-concept and his relationship with school that will take longer to repair than the inconvenience of a classroom change early in the year.

One more pattern in difficult teacher situations: some ADHD children begin to internalize the teacher's assessment of them. A child who hears repeatedly from an adult authority that his behavior is a choice, that he is lazy, or that he could do better if he simply tried harder, begins to incorporate those assessments into his self-concept. He is not just having a bad year. He is building a story about who he is as a learner. Catching and correcting this internalization at home, specifically and repeatedly, is the parent's most important job during a difficult teacher year: keeping the narrative about the ADHD, not about his character.

Communicating With School Staff Without Burning Bridges

The school relationship is a multi-year relationship with people who will have direct daily impact on your son's life. Every communication you send builds or erodes the relational foundation on which that impact rests. This is not an abstract principle. The parent who sends an accusatory email in response to a report card comment on a Tuesday evening will feel the effects of that email through every interaction with that teacher for the remainder of the year.

Email is the dominant communication channel with teachers, and it is a medium that rewards slowness. The most effective school emails are brief, specific, and without emotional charge. They describe a situation, ask a question or make a request, and close without editorializing. Emails that are long, that include multiple grievances, that quote back the teacher's previous communications in a way that implies reproach, or that copy administrators unnecessarily communicate hostility even when that is not the intent. The teacher who receives that email does not think "this parent has a point." They think "this is going to be a difficult year."

The rule for any email written in response to something upsetting is a waiting period of at least several hours, preferably overnight. What you write at ten in the evening after reading a teacher's comment about your son's behavior is almost never what you would write the next morning. The waiting period is not about suppressing your response. It is about separating the emotional event from the communication that represents you and your son in the school system for the duration of the year.

Documentation of school communications serves a different purpose than documentation of incidents: it maintains continuity in a relationship that has many participants and where institutional memory is limited. A brief folder of sent emails, meeting notes, and agreed commitments means that when a teacher says "I don't recall agreeing to that," you have the record. It also means that when you change teachers, you have a summary of what worked that you can share with the new teacher at the beginning of the year, rather than starting from nothing.

Knowing when to copy an administrator on a communication is a judgment call that many parents get wrong in both directions. Copying the principal on every email to a teacher signals that you do not trust the teacher to respond to direct communication, which is accurate in some cases but creates an adversarial dynamic in most. Not copying anyone ever means that when you need to escalate, there is no documented record of prior attempts at direct resolution. The practical guideline is: communicate directly until direct communication has demonstrably failed to produce change, then involve one additional level with explicit reference to the prior direct attempts.

Hold this explicitly: every person in the school system is someone your son will encounter again. The teacher this year may be the department head next year. The counselor who seemed unhelpful may be the one who makes the call that matters when your son is struggling in ninth grade. The investment in relationships that remain functional even through disagreement is not naive. It is long-term thinking in a context where the long term matters more than any individual interaction.

There is a final skill worth naming: knowing when to acknowledge your own mistakes in a school communication. If you sent an email that was sharper than it should have been, a brief follow-up that says "I realize my last message was more pointed than it needed to be. I was frustrated, and I appreciate your patience" resets the interaction more effectively than anything else you could do. Teachers are human, they understand frustration, and they respond to genuine accountability with more generosity than most parents expect. The parent who can repair their own communication errors creates more goodwill than the parent who has never made them.

Chapter 15: IEPs, 504 Plans, and Educational Advocacy

Advocacy is not about fighting. It is about knowing what your child needs and asking for it clearly.

The first time most parents of children with ADHD encounter the formal special education system, they walk into a room with six people sitting across from them, a stack of documents they have never seen before, and a set of acronyms they were not told would be on the agenda. IEP. 504. FAPE. LRE. BIP. The meeting has a specific vocabulary, a specific structure, and a specific set of legal obligations that none of these parents were handed a guide to. They are expected to participate meaningfully in decisions that will shape their son's education for the next year, in a language they were not taught.

This chapter is that guide. It will not turn you into a special education attorney, and it is not trying to. It will give you enough understanding of the system to know what you are entitled to, what to ask for, what the documents mean, and what to do when the school's answer is no. The system is navigable. It is more navigable when you are not walking into it for the first time with no map.

The Difference Between an IEP and a 504 Plan

The confusion between an IEP and a 504 plan is one of the most common sources of disorientation for parents entering the special education system, and the confusion is understandable because both documents involve the school making specific commitments to support a child with a disability. The difference is in the legal framework, the eligibility criteria, and what the document actually does.

A 504 plan takes its name from Section 504 of the Rehabilitation Act of 1973, a federal civil rights law that prohibits discrimination against people with disabilities in programs that receive federal funding, which includes public schools. For a child to be eligible for a 504 plan, the school must determine that the child has a physical or mental impairment that substantially limits one or more major life activities. Learning and concentrating are explicitly listed as major life activities. ADHD, when it substantially limits a child's ability to learn or concentrate, qualifies as an impairment under this definition. The 504 plan documents the accommodations the school will provide to give the child equal access to education. It does not change the curriculum, the standards, or what the child is expected to learn. It changes the conditions under which the child accesses the learning.

An IEP, or Individualized Education Program, operates under a different federal law: the Individuals with Disabilities Education Act (IDEA). To be eligible for an IEP, the child must have a disability that falls within one of IDEA's thirteen specified categories and, crucially, that disability must adversely affect the child's educational performance in a way that requires specially designed instruction. The IEP does more than document accommodations. It establishes specific educational goals, defines specially designed instruction to be provided by qualified special education personnel, and carries a set of procedural rights for parents that is more extensive than those attached to a 504 plan.

For children with ADHD, which plan is appropriate depends on the severity of the impact on educational functioning. A child whose ADHD affects concentration and work completion, but who is performing at or near grade level with accommodations, is typically a 504 candidate. A child whose ADHD co-occurs with a learning disability or whose educational performance is significantly below grade level in ways that require modification of the instructional program itself is more likely to need an IEP. The distinction is not always obvious, and schools sometimes steer parents toward the less resource-intensive option even when the more intensive one would be appropriate. Understanding which document does what is the foundation for knowing what to request.

There is a third document that parents sometimes encounter and should know by name: the Behavior Intervention Plan, or BIP. A BIP is a component of an IEP developed when a child's behavior interferes with learning, either their own or others'. It documents the specific behaviors of concern, the function those behaviors serve, and the proactive strategies and supports the school will provide. A BIP is not a punishment plan. It is a support plan built on a functional analysis of why the behavior is occurring. For a child with ADHD whose behavior in the classroom is generating disciplinary responses, requesting a functional behavioral assessment and the development of a BIP shifts the framework from "how do we stop this behavior" to "what does this child need in order to behave differently," which is a significantly more productive question.

Both plans must be reviewed annually and can be revised when a child's needs change. Both travel with the child when families move to a new school district. The portability of these documents is one of their most practical features: a family that has spent two years establishing the right accommodations does not lose them when they move, as long as the receiving district has time to review and the parent advocates for continuity.

One practical implication of understanding the IEP/504 distinction is knowing which to request in the first place. Many parents, unfamiliar with the system, accept whatever the school offers rather than requesting what is appropriate. A school that offers a 504 plan when a child's needs actually require an IEP is offering a less comprehensive form of support, with fewer procedural protections for the parent and less intensive service delivery. The parent who knows the distinction can ask the right question: does my son need accommodations to access the standard curriculum, or does he need the curriculum or instruction itself to be modified? The answer determines which document is the right one.

How to Request an Evaluation and What to Expect

The formal process for obtaining either an IEP or a 504 plan begins with a request for an educational evaluation. This request is the moment at which legal timelines begin and the school's obligations become enforceable. Understanding what those timelines are and what the obligations entail changes the parent's position from suppliant to participant with rights.

The most important thing to know about the evaluation request is that it must be made in writing. A verbal conversation with a teacher or principal about your concerns, however detailed and sincere, does not trigger the legal process. An email or letter to the school's special education coordinator or principal, stating clearly that you are requesting an evaluation of your son for special education eligibility, does. From the date the school receives that written request, federal law under IDEA gives the school sixty days to complete the evaluation, though some states have different timelines. The school must provide you with a written notice of its response: either that it agrees to evaluate and describes what the evaluation will include, or that it refuses to evaluate and explains why.

If the school declines to evaluate, that refusal must be in writing and must explain the basis for the refusal. You have the right to contest a refusal through the formal dispute channels described later in this chapter. Many parents who receive a verbal suggestion to wait, to give the child another year, or to see how things develop do not realize that they can make the written request regardless of the school's informal recommendation. The formal request and the informal conversation are separate channels, and the formal channel carries legal weight that the informal one does not.

The evaluation itself, when the school agrees to conduct one, must be comprehensive and must assess all areas of suspected disability. For ADHD, this typically includes cognitive and academic assessments, behavioral rating scales completed by teachers and parents, review of existing records, and classroom observation. The evaluation must be conducted by qualified personnel and must not be limited to a single standardized test. If you believe the school's evaluation is insufficient or biased, you have the right to request an Independent Educational Evaluation at the school's expense, a right described in the parental rights section of this chapter.

Once the evaluation is complete, the school must hold a meeting to review the results with you and determine eligibility. This meeting is where the documented evidence from the evaluation is used to determine whether the child meets the criteria for special education services. You are a required participant in this meeting, not a witness. Your input on your son's functioning at home, your observations from previous evaluations, and your knowledge of what works for him are all relevant and should be part of the eligibility discussion.

Preparation for this meeting follows the same logic as preparation for any consequential school meeting: bring concrete observations, write down your questions in advance, and request the evaluation documents before the meeting rather than reading them for the first time in the room.

One specific preparation step that changes what you can contribute to the eligibility meeting is completing your portion of any behavioral rating scales the school sends home before reviewing the school's completed forms. Your independent assessment of your son's functioning at home, completed before you see how the teacher and school rated him, provides uncontaminated data about how his ADHD manifests in a different setting. Children with ADHD frequently present differently at home and at school, and the discrepancy itself is diagnostically relevant. A child who is significantly more regulated at home than at school may be experiencing a particularly poor environmental fit with the classroom structure. A child who is more dysregulated at home may be expending regulatory resources at school to maintain compliance and arriving home depleted. Neither pattern is unusual, and both provide useful information that shapes what the appropriate support looks like. A parent who has completed their ratings independently and can speak to specific home observations brings different information to the table than a parent who simply agrees or disagrees with what the teacher rated.

What to Say and What to Ask at the IEP Meeting

The IEP meeting is the formal annual review of a child's special education program. It is attended by the child's parents, at least one general education teacher, at least one special education teacher, a school representative who can commit resources, and someone who can interpret the evaluation results. It is also the meeting where the school presents a document that the parent is asked to sign.

You do not have to sign anything at the IEP meeting. This is one of the most important pieces of information parents do not receive. The document presented at the meeting is a draft. You are entitled to take it home, review it carefully, consult with someone outside the meeting, and return with your response. A school that pressures you to sign at the meeting is operating outside the spirit of the law, which requires meaningful parental participation rather than rubber-stamp approval. Asking for time to review is not confrontational. It is your legal right.

Before the meeting, request the draft IEP at least forty-eight hours in advance so you have time to read it. Review each goal for specificity: a measurable goal states what the child will do, under what conditions, to what level of accuracy, by when. "Will improve reading fluency" is not a measurable goal. "Given grade-level text, will read 120 words per minute with 95% accuracy by June of the current school year" is. When goals are vague, ask during the meeting how progress will be measured and reported, and who is responsible for each objective.

Review the services section with the same specificity. The document should state how many minutes per week of each service will be provided, by whom, in what setting, and starting when. If the document says "reading support as needed," that is not a commitment. Ask what "as needed" means in practice and ensure the answer is reflected in the written document before you sign.

The questions that generate the most useful information at IEP meetings are concrete and forward-looking: "How will you measure progress on this goal and how often will you report it to me?" "What will happen if my son is not making adequate progress toward this goal by February?" "Who is the primary contact for questions about service delivery?" "If he transitions to a new classroom mid-year, what happens to these services?" These questions signal that you are an informed participant and that you will hold the school accountable for what the document promises.

There is one section of the IEP that parents often review least carefully and that has the most practical daily impact: the section on accommodations and modifications in the general education classroom. This section specifies what every teacher in every classroom is required to do for your son, not just the special education teacher. It is the document that follows him from class to class in middle school and that a substitute teacher should receive when the regular teacher is absent. The accommodations listed here should be specific enough to be implementable by someone who has never met your son. If the section says "extended time" without specifying how much, or "preferential seating" without specifying away from what, those accommodations are too vague to be consistently implemented or monitored. Request specific language before you sign: "time and a half on all assessments" and "front-row seating away from the door and windows" are implementable. Vague language gives the school flexibility that works against your son when teachers interpret it minimally.

Bring someone with you if the meeting feels overwhelming or if you are in a contentious period with the school. A partner, a trusted friend, an educational advocate, or even a note-taker whose sole job is to write down what is said changes the dynamic of the meeting and gives you a record that cannot be disputed later.

Your Legal Rights as a Parent and How to Use Them

The Individuals with Disabilities Education Act establishes a specific set of rights for parents of children receiving special education services. These rights exist because Congress recognized that parents are essential partners in the education of children with disabilities, not optional participants whose involvement schools can choose to accept or decline. Knowing these rights does not make you a litigious parent. It makes you an informed one.

The right to prior written notice means the school must inform you in writing before it makes any change to your son's educational placement, services, or identification as a child with a disability, and before it refuses to make a change you have requested. The notice must explain the basis for the school's decision and reference the information it relied on. A school that changes a child's placement, reduces his services, or removes him from special education without providing this notice is violating your procedural rights, regardless of whether the substantive decision might have been appropriate.

The right to an Independent Educational Evaluation means that if you disagree with the school's evaluation of your son, you can request that an independent evaluator assess him, and the school is required to either fund that evaluation or explain in a hearing why its own evaluation was appropriate. The IEE is a significant right because it means you are not captive to a single source of assessment data, particularly in cases where you believe the school's evaluation minimized your son's needs.

The right to participate in placement decisions means that the IEP team, which includes you, makes placement decisions collaboratively. A school that presents a placement as predetermined and presents the IEP meeting as a formality for communicating that decision is not operating within the law. Your consent is required for initial placement in special education and for changes to placement. For other IEP decisions, your meaningful participation is required even when your consent is not.

Prior to exercising formal dispute rights, most situations are most efficiently addressed through direct communication with the special education director, who typically has more authority and broader context than individual teachers or building-level administrators. Knowing that the formal rights exist gives you standing in that conversation that you would not otherwise have.

There is one parental right that few parents know exists and that is among the most practically significant: the right to request, in writing, a copy of all educational records pertaining to your son. Under the Family Educational Rights and Privacy Act (FERPA), the school must provide those records within forty-five days of the request. This includes evaluation reports, progress notes, disciplinary records, emails between school staff that discuss your son, and meeting notes. Parents who have requested these records before a contentious meeting report finding information that significantly changed their understanding of the situation. The request for records is not an accusation. It is the exercise of a right that Congress determined parents should have, precisely because it creates accountability in a system where parents are otherwise dependent on what the school chooses to share.

The right to an interpreter or translator, if English is not your primary language, is also established in IDEA and must be provided at no cost to the parent. The right to participate meaningfully in your son's education cannot be realized if participation requires fluency in a language you do not speak.

One common misconception about parental rights in special education is that exercising them will damage the relationship with the school. In practice, the opposite is more often true. Schools respond to parents who demonstrate knowledge of the legal framework with more institutional care than they bring to interactions with parents who appear unaware that a framework exists. The parent who sends a written request for records, who asks for prior written notice before any placement change, and who confirms meeting agreements in writing is communicating that they are paying attention and will hold the school accountable. This is not confrontational. It is the behavior of an informed participant, and institutions generally respond to informed participants more carefully than to uninformed ones.

When the School Pushes Back and What You Can Do

Schools push back for a range of reasons, not all of which reflect bad faith. Limited resources, different professional judgments about what a child needs, and genuine disagreement about the appropriate interpretation of evaluation data are all common sources of conflict that do not require an adversarial response. Other pushbacks reflect institutional inertia, procedural shortcuts, or, in some cases, active resistance to providing services that have real cost implications. Distinguishing between these categories determines what response is proportionate.

The documentation practice established in Chapter 14 is the foundation of effective advocacy when conflict arises. A parent who has a written record of what was requested, what the school responded, and what was observed in the classroom is in a fundamentally different position from a parent who is relying on memory of conversations. Specific, dated documentation of incidents where IEP goals were not implemented, services were not delivered, or procedural rights were not followed is the evidence that makes a formal complaint or dispute resolution actionable rather than merely asserted.

The escalation sequence for school pushback follows a specific order for practical reasons. The first step is a direct, written communication to the special education coordinator or director laying out the specific concern and requesting a response within a defined timeframe, typically ten business days. If that communication does not produce a satisfactory response, the next step is a request for a formal IEP meeting to address the issue, not a general conversation. Formal meetings generate written records and require written responses.

If the IEP meeting does not resolve the conflict, federal and state laws provide several formal options: state complaint, which is filed with the state education agency and triggers an investigation with a required resolution timeline; mediation, which is a voluntary process in which a neutral mediator helps both parties reach agreement; and due process, which is a formal legal proceeding before an impartial hearing officer. Due process is the most adversarial option and also the most resource-intensive for both parties. Most disputes that warrant formal escalation are resolved through state complaint or mediation before reaching due process.

One practical reality of the special education dispute system is that the formal options, state complaint and due process in particular, have timelines that are incompatible with the urgency of a child's current school year. A state complaint investigation takes sixty days. A due process hearing can take months. Mediation is faster but still requires scheduling and preparation. For issues that need resolution within weeks, not months, the most effective tool is often a well-documented, formally worded letter from the parent to the superintendent's office that describes the violation, references the specific legal provisions, and requests a response within ten business days. The letter signals that this parent knows the law and will use the formal channels if necessary, which frequently produces faster cooperation than the formal channels themselves.

An independent educational advocate is a practical resource at any point in the escalation sequence. Educational advocates are professionals who know the special education system, can help parents understand their rights, review IEP documents for adequacy, attend meetings with parents, and help draft communications. They are not attorneys and cannot represent parents in due process hearings, but for the vast majority of conflicts that do not reach that point, they are more efficient and far less expensive than legal representation. Finding an advocate through a parent advocacy organization in your state is a concrete step available to any parent who is feeling lost in the system.

One final point about conflict with schools: the goal of the advocacy process is never to win. It is to get your son what he needs to succeed in school. A parent who treats every disagreement as a battle to be won tends to accumulate adversaries and to spend energy on the conflict itself instead of on the outcome for the child. The parent who holds the question "what does my son need, and how do I get the school to provide it" at the center of every interaction, pushing aside the question of who is right, maintains the clarity that effective advocacy requires across what is often a multi-year relationship with the same institution.

Chapter 16: ADHD, Anxiety, and What Else Might Be Going On

The most common way people give up their power is by thinking they don't have any.

You already have the diagnosis. You have the strategies. You may have the medication. And yet something still does not quite fit. Your son is responding to some things but not others. There are behaviors that the ADHD framework explains well and behaviors that it does not seem to touch. You find yourself wondering whether you are missing something, whether the picture you were given is the complete one.

You are not catastrophizing. The clinical reality is that ADHD rarely travels alone. Knowing what else might be present is not a sign of anxiety about your son's future. It is the kind of precise thinking that gets children the right support rather than a partial version of it.

Why ADHD Rarely Comes Alone

The statistic that most parents are not given at diagnosis is this: more than sixty percent of children diagnosed with ADHD have at least one co-occurring diagnosable condition. Some estimates, depending on the sample and the diagnostic criteria used, put that figure closer to eighty percent. ADHD is a neurobiological condition that affects the development and functioning of the prefrontal cortex, and the brain systems that ADHD disrupts are not isolated from the systems that regulate emotion, process language, manage anxiety, or support learning. The overlapping vulnerability is not coincidental.

The most commonly co-occurring conditions include anxiety disorders, which appear in roughly fifty percent of children with ADHD; oppositional defiant disorder, present in approximately forty to sixty percent; specific learning disorders including dyslexia, dysgraphia, and dyscalculia; mood disorders including depression and dysthymia; sleep disorders; and, in a subset of children, autism spectrum disorder. These are not rare edge cases that apply to a small population of unusually complex children. They are the statistical norm for a child with ADHD.

The reason this matters clinically is that each condition, when present alongside ADHD, changes what treatment looks like and which strategies are most effective. Medication calibrated for ADHD alone often works only partially when anxiety is also present, because the stimulant medications that reduce ADHD symptoms can also amplify anxiety. Behavioral strategies designed for ADHD-related defiance frequently fail when the behavior is actually driven by an unidentified learning disorder creating chronic frustration and shame. The treatment plan that targets only one condition while the other remains unaddressed is not a failed treatment for a treatment-resistant child. It is the right treatment for half the problem.

There is a version of this that parents encounter specifically with medication. A stimulant medication that reduces hyperactivity and improves focus but does not touch a child's morning dread of school, his refusal to attempt written assignments, or his social withdrawal is doing what it was designed to do for ADHD. The remaining problems are not medication failures. They are signals pointing to conditions the medication was never designed to address.

The frame shift that is most useful for parents is this: a child whose ADHD treatment is working well but who still struggles significantly is not a child who needs more of the same. He is a child who may need a broader diagnostic picture. Recognizing the possibility of co-occurring conditions is not lowering expectations or accumulating labels. It is refusing to stop at an incomplete answer when a more complete one is available and would change how you help him.

There is a specific clinical pattern worth naming that often delays the recognition of co-occurring conditions: what clinicians call diagnostic overshadowing. When a child carries an ADHD diagnosis, new symptoms or behaviors that emerge are frequently attributed to the existing diagnosis rather than prompting consideration of whether something additional is present. A child who develops significant sleep problems is assumed to be experiencing ADHD-related dysregulation. A child whose academic functioning drops sharply is assumed to be having an ADHD attention episode. A child who becomes increasingly withdrawn is assumed to be experiencing ADHD fatigue. Each of these explanations may be correct, but each of them may also be wrong, and the cost of the wrong explanation is that a treatable condition goes unaddressed for months or years while the child accumulates the secondary effects of untreated difficulty.

What makes the identification of comorbidities in children with ADHD particularly difficult is that ADHD itself, as a condition, generates symptoms that overlap with almost every other childhood disorder. Inattention and academic difficulty overlap with learning disorders. Emotional dysregulation and irritability overlap with mood disorders and ODD. Sleep disruption overlaps with anxiety. The diagnostic work of determining what is ADHD and what is something else requires a clinician with specific experience in this overlap, which is one reason a general practitioner who diagnosed ADHD quickly is often not the right person to assess for co-occurring conditions.

Recognizing Anxiety in Boys Who Mask It With Acting Out

The textbook presentation of anxiety in children involves worry, avoidance, physical complaints, and distress that is legible to adults as fear. A child who says "I am worried about the test" or who cries before school or who asks repeatedly whether something bad is going to happen fits the image that most parents and many teachers carry of what an anxious child looks like. Boys with ADHD frequently do not look like this, and the mismatch between expectation and presentation is one of the most consequential missed diagnoses in this population.

For many boys, anxiety manifests not as withdrawal or verbalized worry but as aggression, explosiveness, refusal, and avoidance dressed up as defiance. A child who refuses to go to soccer practice is not necessarily being oppositional. He may be managing a social anxiety about performance that he does not have the vocabulary to name. A child who melts down every morning before school may not primarily have a regulation problem. He may have a profound anxiety about what the day will bring, expressed through the only channel available to him. A child who becomes aggressive when asked to try something new may not be defiant. He may be terrified of failure in a way that looks nothing like fear.

The behavioral signals that suggest anxiety rather than, or in addition to, ADHD-related dysregulation include a pattern of avoidance that is situationally specific, meaning it clusters around particular contexts and not scattered unpredictably across situations; explosive behavior that reliably precedes specific demands or transitions; physical complaints, including stomachaches and headaches, that appear on school days or before challenging events; sleep onset difficulties driven by racing thoughts that the child reports at night; and a need for reassurance that is excessive relative to the situation. The last one is particularly telling: a child who repeatedly checks whether he did something right, whether you are angry with him, or whether something bad is going to happen is expressing anxiety through reassurance-seeking, even when everything else he does looks like impulsivity and defiance.

The clinical significance of identifying anxiety as a co-occurring condition, and not defaulting to an all-ADHD explanation for every behavior, is that the interventions are different. Anxiety responds to gradual exposure, to teaching the child to tolerate and move through uncertain situations, and in many cases to specific therapeutic approaches such as cognitive behavioral therapy that target anxious thought patterns. Simply managing consequences for anxious avoidance without addressing the anxiety itself is likely to increase the distress without reducing the behavior. A child who is avoiding something because he is afraid needs a different response than a child who is avoiding something because he finds it boring.

There is a practical screening question that parents can use as an informal starting point: when your son refuses or explodes, does the situation that triggers it share a common element across different contexts? If the refusals cluster around situations involving evaluation, social comparison, novel environments, or proximity to failure, anxiety is the more likely driver. If they cluster around tasks that are genuinely boring and low in stimulation, ADHD-related motivation deficits are the more likely driver. Both can be present simultaneously, but identifying which is primary in a given pattern of behavior determines which intervention is most likely to help. A parent who has mapped the trigger patterns described in Chapter 11 will already have the data needed to make this distinction.

The reason this distinction has therapeutic consequences is not abstract. Anxiety responds to approaches that help the child tolerate and move through uncertain or feared situations, paired with the understanding that avoidance, while it relieves anxiety in the short term, reliably makes it worse over time. Teaching a child who is driven by boredom avoidance to tolerate discomfort is productive. Teaching a child who is driven by fear avoidance the same skill in isolation, without addressing the fear itself, is asking him to walk toward what he is afraid of without any tools for managing the fear. The clinical word for what he needs is different, and getting the clinical picture right is what makes the intervention work.

Learning Differences That Often Co-Occur With ADHD

Dyslexia is the most common learning disorder co-occurring with ADHD, appearing in an estimated thirty to forty percent of children with ADHD.

Dysgraphia, which affects written expression and handwriting fluency, is present in a similarly elevated proportion. Dyscalculia, which affects mathematical reasoning and number sense, co-occurs at rates substantially higher than in the general population. Auditory processing disorder, which affects the child's ability to accurately process and interpret spoken language despite normal hearing, is identified in a significant subset of children with ADHD and is frequently missed because hearing tests come back normal.

The practical problem for parents is that ADHD alone, without any co-occurring learning disorder, produces significant academic difficulty. Inattention, poor working memory, weak executive function, and difficulty sustaining effort on tasks that are not intrinsically interesting account for a great deal of underperformance in school. It is genuinely difficult to know, watching a child struggle to read, whether the struggle is coming from attention difficulties making it hard to focus on text, from an underlying phonological processing deficit that affects decoding, or from both simultaneously.

The clinical distinction that matters most for treatment is this: ADHD-related reading difficulties tend to be inconsistent and variable with engagement and interest. A child who reads well in a high-interest context but poorly in a low-interest one is showing the attentional signature. A child who struggles with decoding consistently, regardless of interest level, who confuses similar-looking letters or words, who has particular difficulty sounding out new words, and who has a family history of reading difficulties is showing signals that warrant evaluation for dyslexia specifically.

The same logic applies to written expression. A child who writes slowly but whose composition, when it finally appears on the page, is reasonably organized and syntactically intact is showing the output difficulty typical of ADHD. A child whose written work shows consistent spelling errors, reversed letters, difficulty forming letters fluently, and a marked discrepancy between what he can say aloud and what he can produce in writing warrants evaluation for dysgraphia.

When a learning disorder is present alongside ADHD, the IEP must address both conditions, not just the ADHD. Accommodations designed for ADHD, such as extended time and reduced distraction, do not constitute appropriate support for a reading disorder that requires explicit phonological instruction. A child who has both conditions and receives only ADHD accommodations is receiving half the support his documented profile requires. This is a specific, actionable point worth raising with the IEP team if the evaluation has identified learning disorders that are not reflected in the service plan.

One consequence of unidentified learning disorders in children with ADHD that deserves direct acknowledgment is shame. A child who struggles to read and does not know why, who works as hard as other children and produces less, who watches peers move forward while he remains behind, accumulates a narrative about himself that is deeply corrosive. He concludes that he is not trying hard enough, that he is not smart enough, or that something is fundamentally wrong with him that effort cannot fix. This narrative forms before he has any framework for understanding what is actually happening in his brain. Identifying the learning disorder and naming it accurately, "your brain processes written language differently, and here is what we do about that," interrupts the narrative. It gives him an explanation that is accurate rather than self-blaming, and it is the foundation on which appropriate remediation can be built.

For dyslexia specifically, there is now substantial evidence that structured literacy approaches, built on explicit phonological awareness instruction, produce meaningful gains in reading fluency when implemented consistently and with fidelity. This is not a reading enrichment program or a tutoring supplement. It is a specific instructional approach that requires trained practitioners and sufficient instructional time. If your son has been evaluated for dyslexia, asking the school whether the reading instruction in his IEP is a structured literacy program is a specific, answerable question that will tell you a great deal about whether the intervention matches the need.

When to Seek Additional Evaluation and Support

The question of when a child's presentation warrants looking beyond the initial ADHD diagnosis is not one that has a single bright-line answer, but there are specific patterns that should prompt the conversation with a qualified clinician. The most reliable indicator is a response to treatment that is partial but not complete: medication that reduces hyperactivity and improves attention but does not touch the anxiety-driven avoidance or the learning-based frustration. A treatment plan that is working exactly as designed for ADHD but leaving significant problems unaddressed is pointing you toward something the ADHD diagnosis is not capturing.

Other indicators include behaviors that are disproportionate to the child's ADHD profile as you understand it. If you have a solid sense of what ADHD looks like in your son and you are observing something that does not fit that pattern, that observation is worth taking seriously. A significant regression after a period of relative stability, a new onset of persistent physical complaints, a change in sleep patterns that is not explained by environmental changes, or a qualitative shift in how your son talks about himself, including increasing statements of self-blame, shame, or worthlessness, all warrant clinical attention beyond the existing diagnostic framework.

The right professional for a comprehensive evaluation of co-occurring conditions depends on what you suspect is present. A child psychiatrist has the broadest scope to assess and treat the full range of psychiatric co-occurring conditions including mood disorders, anxiety disorders, and ODD. A neuropsychologist is the most appropriate clinician for a comprehensive assessment that includes cognitive, academic, and behavioral domains, and is particularly well-suited when learning disorders are suspected. A clinical psychologist with experience in child anxiety is appropriate when the presenting concern is primarily anxiety rather than learning differences. The family's pediatrician or the clinician who made the initial ADHD diagnosis can help triage the referral, but should not be the end point of the assessment if co-occurring conditions are suspected.

One thing that stops parents from requesting additional evaluation is the concern that asking for it implies that the current treatment or the initial diagnosis was a failure. It is not. The initial diagnosis identified what was most prominent and most impairing at the time it was conducted. Co-occurring conditions are sometimes not apparent until the primary ADHD symptoms are better managed and the underlying layer becomes more visible. A child whose ADHD was so dominant that it obscured everything else at age seven may, at age ten with medication managing the core symptoms, begin to show the anxiety or learning differences that were always present but masked. Seeking a more complete picture is not undoing the original diagnosis. It is building on it.

One practical step before requesting a formal evaluation is to document the specific pattern you are observing and bring it to the appointment. A description of "he is struggling" gives the clinician little to work with. A description of "he refuses to go to baseball practice specifically, not other activities; the refusal began in March after a game where he struck out in the ninth inning; he has trouble sleeping on

Sunday nights before school; he reports stomachaches on Monday mornings" gives the clinician a pattern to assess. The more specific and behaviorally anchored the information you bring, the more efficient the evaluation will be.

The timing question is also worth addressing directly: there is no clinical benefit to waiting until a co-occurring condition becomes more severe before seeking evaluation. The argument for waiting is understandable: "let's see if he grows out of it," or "maybe it's just a phase," or "we don't want to overwhelm him with more appointments." Each of these feels reasonable. Each carries a cost. The months and years during which a child experiences unidentified anxiety, unidentified dyslexia, or unidentified depression are months and years of accumulated difficulty that shapes his relationship with school, with himself, and with the adults around him. Early identification and targeted support produce better outcomes than later identification of the same conditions, across virtually every co-occurring condition that presents with ADHD.

Managing Multiple Diagnoses Without Losing Your Mind

The practical reality of parenting a child with multiple diagnoses is that the systems designed to support children rarely communicate with each other at the level the child actually needs. The psychiatrist who manages the medication knows the neurological piece. The psychologist providing CBT knows the behavioral and emotional piece. The special education team at school knows the academic piece. None of these professionals has a complete view of the child, and none of them is going to coordinate with the others unless someone makes that happen. That someone is you.

The parent's role as care coordinator is one of the most demanding and least acknowledged aspects of raising a child with complex needs. It involves maintaining a current summary of your son's diagnoses, current medications and dosages, active therapeutic interventions, and academic accommodations in a single document that you can share with any new provider, so you are not starting from scratch at every intake appointment. It involves communicating relevant information between providers when one makes a change that is likely to affect another's domain: when the psychiatrist adjusts the medication, the school and the psychologist need to know, because the behavioral patterns they are tracking will shift. When the school observes a significant change in academic functioning, the psychiatrist and psychologist need that data.

Prioritizing treatment when multiple conditions are present requires a practical framework rather than an attempt to address everything simultaneously. The general clinical principle is to begin with the condition that is most impairing and most likely to respond to treatment, address that first, then reassess what remains. Severe anxiety that is making it impossible for a child to attend school is a higher priority than optimizing attention medication, because attending school is the prerequisite for everything else. A learning disorder that is generating escalating shame and refusal is a higher priority than working on social skills, because the shame is fueling the behavioral problems in other domains. The sequencing is determined by what is most impairing right now, not by what feels most manageable.

The internal resource that matters most in this coordination role is the ability to hold the full picture of your son while each specialist holds only their piece. This is not a skill that comes with the territory. It develops over time, through experience with the systems involved and through the hard work of synthesizing information from multiple professional perspectives into a coherent understanding of one particular child. No professional, regardless of how skilled or caring, can do this for you. You are the only person who has seen your son across every context, every year of his life, every bad day and every unexpectedly good one. That perspective has clinical value, and using it actively is not overstepping. It is doing exactly what the situation requires.

The coordination role also includes knowing when a provider relationship is not working. A psychiatrist who dismisses your observation that the medication change produced a significant behavioral shift, a therapist whose approach has not produced any measurable progress after six months, a school that continues to attribute documented anxiety to willful defiance, are all situations that warrant a direct conversation and, if the conversation produces nothing, a change in provider. Parents of children with complex needs sometimes remain with unhelpful providers out of exhaustion or deference to professional authority. The child's outcomes are the metric that matters, and a provider who is not contributing to improvement in those outcomes needs to change.

One structural tool that helps manage the complexity of multiple providers is a brief written summary, one or two pages, that you update every six months and share with any new professional involved in your son's care. It covers the diagnoses, the current treatment plan, what is working, what is not, and the specific questions you are trying to answer at this stage. Providers who receive this document at intake report that it shortens the time to useful clinical engagement significantly. More importantly, it signals that you are an organized, informed parent who will be a reliable partner in the treatment, which tends to raise the quality of the professional engagement you receive in return.

Chapter 17:
Raising a Boy Who Believes in Himself

It is not our abilities that show what we truly are. It is our choices.

There is a fear that most parents of boys with ADHD carry but rarely say out loud. It is not the fear about grades or friendships or whether the medication is right. It is more specific and more painful than any of those. It is the fear that the daily accumulation of difficulty, the corrections, the frustrated teachers, the homework battles, the moments when he looks at other kids and can see that something is different about him, is building a story inside your son. And that the story says: I am the problem. I am not enough. I am the kind of person things do not work out for.

That fear is not irrational. Research consistently finds that children with ADHD receive significantly more negative feedback from adults than their peers, across settings and across years. What this chapter addresses is how to interrupt that accumulation before it becomes the foundation of how your son sees himself, and how to build something more accurate and more durable in its place.

The Hidden Shame ADHD Boys Carry

There is an important distinction in clinical psychology between guilt and shame, and it matters in a practical way for understanding what many boys with ADHD are carrying. Guilt is the feeling that you did something bad. Shame is the feeling that you are something bad. Guilt is specific and bounded: it attaches to an action and, at least in principle, can be resolved by repairing what was done. Shame is diffuse and self-defining: it attaches to identity and does not resolve with a single repair because it is not about a single action. It is about who you believe yourself to be.

A child with ADHD who has spent years being called out in class, who has watched his parents exhale with frustration at the dinner table, who has been pulled aside by coaches and teachers and principals, who has heard "you're so smart, you just need to try harder" often enough to know that the sentence is a reprimand with compliment packaging, is not accumulating guilt. He is accumulating shame. He is not concluding "I did that wrong today." He is concluding "I am the kind of person who does things wrong." That is a more durable and more damaging belief, and it does not respond to praise, reward charts, or motivation strategies alone.

The neurological component of this shame pattern deserves acknowledgment. Executive function deficits mean that a child with ADHD genuinely cannot perform certain tasks as reliably as his peers, even when he wants to, even when the consequences of not doing so are significant, even when he has been told clearly what is expected. Years of failing to meet expectations he genuinely intended to meet produces a specific kind of shame: not the shame of not trying, but the shame of trying and still failing. This is qualitatively different from the experience of a child who underperforms because he does not care. It is more painful and more persistent.

The first step in working with this accumulated shame is not to address it directly with reassurance or to layer positive experiences over it before the negative ones have been acknowledged. A child who is told he is wonderful while the internal evidence of his daily experience tells him otherwise will not update toward the positive feedback. He will distrust it, or he will accept it briefly and then return to the shame baseline when the next difficulty arrives. Before you can build on top of something, you have to acknowledge what is there. That acknowledgment begins with understanding where the shame came from and naming it accurately.

One of the more painful dimensions of accumulated ADHD shame is that it frequently goes unacknowledged by the adults in the child's life, not because those adults do not care, but because the shame is not visible in a form that reads as distress. It presents as bravado, as indifference, as acting out, as refusal to try new things. A child who says "I don't care about that anyway" when he fails is often protecting himself from shame, not expressing genuine disinterest. A child who becomes aggressive when he makes a mistake is often displacing shame rather than expressing anger. The behavior that adults see, and often respond to with discipline, is the outer layer of an internal experience that the child may not yet have language for.

The adults who consistently correct, redirect, and discipline a child with ADHD are rarely acting out of malice. They are responding to real behavior that creates real problems in real classrooms. But the cumulative effect of those responses on the child who receives them, even when each individual response is proportionate and professionally appropriate, is a relentless signal that he is the source of disruption.

Over a school year, that signal arrives hundreds of times. Over several years, it builds something in the child's internal self-concept that does not disappear when the corrections stop.

Understanding the difference between "you struggled with that" and "you are a struggling person" is the cognitive work that underlies almost everything else in this chapter. The first is a specific observation about a specific situation. The second is an identity conclusion. Your son has been making identity conclusions from situational evidence for years. Your job is to interrupt that pattern with precision, not with blanket reassurance.

Shifting From a Problem-Focused to a Strengths-Based View

The strengths-based approach to ADHD is sometimes understood as a motivational technique or a way to make children feel better about themselves. It is actually a more accurate framework. The characteristics associated with ADHD do not disappear in a strengths-based view. They are understood differently: as traits that function poorly in certain contexts and function well in others, rather than as flaws that would ideally be eliminated.

Impulsivity and creative generation share neural circuitry. The same reduced inhibitory control that makes it difficult for a child to wait his turn in a classroom discussion allows him to make cognitive leaps that slower-processing, more inhibited thinkers do not make. This is not a consolation prize. Studies examining creative problem-solving in populations with ADHD consistently find elevated performance on divergent thinking tasks relative to neurotypical peers. The creativity is real. What is also real is that it does not compensate for the impulsivity in every context, and it should not be deployed as a reframe in moments when the impulsivity has caused genuine harm.

Hyperfocus is the characteristic most frequently cited in strengths-based discussions, and it is worth understanding clearly. The same attention system that fails to sustain engagement on low-stimulation tasks can lock onto a high-interest task with an intensity that most neurotypical children cannot replicate. A child who hyperfocuses on building something, on a sport, on a game, on a creative project, is demonstrating a form of deep attentional capacity that is genuinely unusual. The challenge is that the child usually cannot direct the hyperfocus by choice; it attaches to what his interest system selects. The parent's role in working with hyperfocus is not to manufacture it, but to notice where it naturally occurs and to treat those observations as data about who the child is and what environments allow him to function best.

The practical work of shifting to a strengths-based view requires specificity. Generic reassurance ("you're so creative!") does not build genuine self-knowledge. Specific observations do. "I noticed that when you were building that model last week, you worked for two hours without stopping, and when you hit the part that wasn't working, you found three different ways to fix it before you got one that worked." That sentence describes real observed behavior. It tells the child something concrete about how he functions when the context is right. Over time, specific observations accumulate into an internal picture that the child can carry into difficult situations: "I know I can solve hard problems when I am working on something I care about."

The practical work of identifying strengths also involves paying attention to what your son does when he is not being managed. When left to his own devices, what does he choose to do? What problems does he voluntarily spend time on? What subjects can he talk about at length without losing interest? These voluntary engagement patterns reveal the interest and motivation architecture of his particular brain, and they are a far more reliable guide to genuine strengths than any formal assessment. A child who builds elaborate mechanical structures in his free time is showing you something about his spatial reasoning and his tolerance for iterative problem-solving. A child who organizes the neighborhood kids into elaborate games with complex rules is showing you something about his social creativity and his capacity for systems thinking. These are real competencies that most adults around him are not documenting because they appear in contexts that do not generate formal grades or official recognition.

The identification of real strengths also requires distinguishing between what a child does well by comparison to his ADHD baseline and what he does well by comparison to any external standard. Both are worth acknowledging, but they are different. A child who is significantly better at managing his frustration than he was eight months ago has made real progress worth naming. It is not the same as being a child who manages frustration well by general standards. Collapsing the distinction does the child a disservice in both directions: it minimizes real progress, and it creates false expectations that set him up for another disappointment.

How to Build Resilience Without Minimizing the Hard Parts

The fastest way to teach a child not to come to you when things are hard is to respond to his hard things by minimizing them. "It's not that bad." "Everyone struggles sometimes." "You'll be fine." Each of these sentences, said with genuine love, teaches the child that the gap between his experience and what the adult can tolerate hearing is too wide to bridge. He learns to manage his distress privately rather than bring it to a relationship where it will be reduced before it has been acknowledged.

Genuine resilience is not the absence of distress. It is the capacity to experience distress and continue functioning, to come through a hard experience with your sense of self intact and with some understanding of how you got through it. This capacity develops through supported exposure to difficulty, not through the removal of difficulty or the minimization of its reality. A child who has been told "you've got this" before every hard thing and has sometimes not gotten it learns that the reassurance is not connected to reality. A child who has been told "this is going to be hard, and here's how we'll think about it together" has a different internal resource to draw on.

The language that builds resilience in children with ADHD is language that separates the difficulty from the identity conclusion. "That was really hard" is not "you struggled because of who you are." "You didn't finish it today, and tomorrow we'll try a different approach" is not "you failed." "I can see this is frustrating" acknowledges the reality of the experience without either minimizing it or escalating it into a catastrophe. The consistent use of this language over months and years builds a child who can observe his own difficulty without immediately converting it into a self-indictment.

The timing of the resilience-building conversation matters as much as its content. Attempting to reframe a difficulty while the child is still in the acute distress of it is not going to work. A child who has just received a failing grade, who has just had a public meltdown, or who has just been told he cannot attend a social event because of his behavior is not in a cognitive state that can absorb perspective. What he needs in that moment is acknowledgment, not reframing. "That really hurt" is the right response to acute pain. The conversation about what comes next, about what can be learned or adjusted, happens later, in the recovery window when the child's nervous system is regulated enough to think clearly and respond.

Parents who try to compress the acknowledgment and the reframe into a single exchange often find that the child shuts down or escalates. This is not resistance to the parent's help. It is the nervous system telling the parent that the timing is wrong. The willingness to wait, to let the acute distress pass before moving to problem-solving, is itself a form of respect for the child's experience that teaches him something about how to manage difficulty: first you feel it, then you think about it.

There is a specific pattern in children with ADHD called negative self-talk that develops from the accumulated shame described in the first section of this chapter and that becomes, in adolescence, one of the most significant risk factors for depression and anxiety. The child who at age eight says "I'm stupid" when he makes a mistake is showing an early form of this pattern. The response that builds resilience is not "no you're not, you're very smart." It is "that sounds like the mean voice talking. What actually happened?" This distinction redirects the child from the identity conclusion to the specific event, which is observable and specific and therefore something he can think about clearly.

Helping Your Son Develop His Own Identity Beyond ADHD

There is a well-documented risk in families of children with significant diagnoses: the diagnosis gradually becomes the organizing framework for everything. Conversations about the child center on the diagnosis. Decisions about activities, schools, and social opportunities are filtered primarily through the diagnosis. The child learns, through years of this framing, that the most important thing about him, the thing that explains everything about how his life works, is his ADHD. This is not the lesson that serves him.

ADHD is one characteristic among many that your son has. It is a significant one, with real implications for how he learns, regulates, and relates to others. It is also not the whole picture, and treating it as the whole picture narrows the child's sense of what he is capable of and what he is allowed to be. A boy who has ADHD and is also a gifted builder, a loyal friend, someone who makes people laugh, someone who cares about fairness to a degree that strikes adults as unusual, is a complete person who happens to have a neurological difference. The difference matters, and it is not the defining fact.

The practical work of supporting identity development beyond the diagnosis involves several concrete things. The first is investing in activities and environments where the child's strengths are visible and where the ADHD-related difficulties are less impairing. A child who struggles in a classroom but excels in a workshop, on a basketball court, in a kitchen, or in front of a camera is learning something important about the contexts in which he can function well. That knowledge is part of his identity and should be named explicitly: "You're someone who works well when you can move around and see what you're building."

The question of how and when to talk with your son about his ADHD diagnosis is one that parents navigate differently depending on the child's age, temperament, and the circumstances of the diagnosis. The clinical consensus is that children benefit from accurate, age-appropriate information about their diagnosis rather than from either over-disclosure or concealment. A child who understands that his brain processes certain things differently, that this has specific implications for how he learns and regulates, and that many people with similar brains have done remarkable things, has information that is accurate and that can be integrated into a coherent identity. There is a specific developmental milestone worth naming here: the moment when a child becomes aware of his own difference. For many boys, this happens somewhere between ages seven and ten, when the gap between his experience of school and his peers' experience becomes impossible to ignore. He sees that other kids finish their work when he does not. He sees that other kids do not get pulled aside by the teacher. He sees that other kids do not have to go to a separate room for tests. The awareness of difference is not itself damaging. What is damaging is having no framework for understanding what that difference means.

A child who has a diagnosis and understands it in age-appropriate terms has something to work with. He knows that his brain is wired differently, that this creates specific challenges in specific situations, and that it does not determine his value or his future. This understanding is not a ceiling. It is a floor, a foundation from which he can begin to build a more accurate and more nuanced self-concept than the one available to a child who simply knows that things are harder for him than for everyone else and has no explanation for why.

A child who has never been told anything about his diagnosis, but who has noticed for years that he is treated differently and that school is harder for him than for others, is constructing an explanation for those observations on his own. The explanation he constructs without accurate information is rarely the one you would choose for him.

Celebrating Small Wins in a World That Rewards Big Ones

The educational and social systems in which children grow up are calibrated to recognize and reward visible, standardized achievement. Academic performance is measured against grade-level benchmarks. Athletic achievement is measured against competitive results. Social status involves comparative visibility. For a child with ADHD who may be functioning below grade-level benchmarks, who may not be the highest performer on the team, and whose most significant growth often happens in dimensions that standardized systems do not measure, the external feedback environment is systematically skewed toward the negative.

This is not something you can change about the world your son is growing up in. It is something you can compensate for, deliberately and specifically, within the family environment. The parent who notices and names the progress that the school does not notice is doing something that has direct consequences for the child's self-concept and long-term motivation. The research on intrinsic motivation consistently finds that genuine acknowledgment of effort and process, specific and observed rather than generic and performative, sustains motivation better than rewards attached to outcomes. A child who knows that his effort is seen, regardless of the outcome it produces, develops a different relationship with difficult tasks than a child who only receives feedback on results.

The specific practice of celebrating small wins requires calibrating what counts as a win for your particular son in his current phase of development. For a child who has never been able to transition from homework to dinner without a fight, completing that transition calmly three days in a row is a genuine achievement that deserves genuine acknowledgment. For a child who has historically exploded when losing at games, conceding a loss without an outburst once is worth naming specifically. The calibration has to be accurate to the child's actual baseline, not to what would be unremarkable for a neurotypical child, because the neurotypical standard is the wrong comparison class for measuring his progress.

The language of acknowledgment matters as much as the fact of it. "Good job" is not a useful form of recognition for a child who already suspects that the bar for his "good job" is lower than his peers'. Specific language that describes what was actually observed builds more durable self-knowledge: "You had three tests this week and you came home each day and opened your backpack without me reminding you. That is different from two months ago, and I noticed it." That sentence is specific, accurate, observed, and calibrated to his actual progress. It does not compare him to anyone else. It compares him to his own prior functioning, which is the only comparison that serves him.

There is a meaningful distinction between acknowledging small wins in private and doing so publicly, and the distinction matters for a child who is already sensitive to comparisons with peers. A parent who announces a child's progress to other family members or to the child's friends is well-intentioned but may be creating an additional layer of exposure that the child does not want. Small wins are most powerful when acknowledged in the relationship between parent and child, specifically and privately, not broadcast as a form of social validation. The child who knows that his parent sees his progress, regardless of whether anyone else does, is building something more durable than the child who learns to need external validation for every forward step.

The other dimension of small-win acknowledgment worth addressing is consistency over intensity. A parent who notices progress three times per week for six months is doing more for the child's self-concept than a parent who gives an elaborate acknowledgment once per month. The signal the child needs is not that his progress occasionally produces a significant response. It is that his progress is routinely seen. Routine observation, named quietly and specifically, communicates more than occasional celebration.

Building a system for recognizing small wins does not require a formal reward program or a points chart. It requires attention. It requires that you are watching for the moments when your son does the thing that is hard for him, that you name what you saw when it happens, and that you do it consistently enough that he comes to believe that progress, not just achievement, is something that gets noticed in your family.

Chapter 18: Family Dynamics, Siblings, and the Home Ecosystem

Family is not an important thing. It is everything.

"Why does he always get to do that and I don't?" "Why is it always about him?" "It's not fair." These sentences come from the sibling. They come at the end of a long day, or at the dinner table, or quietly in a moment when the child without ADHD has reached the limit of her patience with a family structure that has, from her perspective, reorganized itself around someone else's needs.

That voice is legitimate. It is not jealousy to be managed away. It is an accurate observation about a real dynamic that exists in most families where one child has ADHD. The disorder does not stay contained in one person. It moves through the household, reshaping routines, redistributing parental attention, generating its own gravitational field that everything else orbits. Acknowledging this honestly is not catastrophizing. It is the starting point for thinking about the family as a whole rather than one of its members.

How ADHD Affects the Whole Family, Not Just One Child

The research on family stress in households with an ADHD child consistently finds elevated levels of parental anxiety, marital strain, and sibling distress relative to families without a child with ADHD. These findings are not surprising to parents who are living them. What is less commonly acknowledged is that the stress is not simply the result of a child's difficult behavior. It is the result of a sustained and demanding management role that falls primarily on the parents, often without adequate external support, in a cultural context that does not consistently recognize the difficulty of what they are doing.

Parental stress in ADHD households operates on multiple channels simultaneously. There is the daily management stress of navigating a child whose behavior is unpredictable and often exhausting. There is the cognitive load of staying on top of medication schedules, school communications, therapy appointments, and IEP meetings. There is the emotional labor of holding space for a child's frustration while managing your own. And there is the grief that many parents carry and rarely name: the grief of watching a child struggle in ways you cannot fully fix, the gap between what you hoped his life would look like and what it actually looks like at this particular moment in time.

This grief is normal and does not indicate inadequate love or insufficient optimism. It is the natural response to sustained difficulty in someone you love, and it deserves the same acknowledgment as every other emotional reality in the household. A parent who does not recognize and process this grief has fewer internal resources available for the daily demands of parenting, because unprocessed emotion takes up the cognitive and emotional bandwidth that is needed for everything else.

The social isolation that many ADHD families experience is another dimension that receives insufficient attention. Playdates that do not get repeated because the child's behavior made them difficult. Family gatherings that become sources of anxiety. Friendships between parents that drift when the difference in parenting experience becomes too wide to bridge. The family that begins to manage its social exposure carefully, limiting situations that are high-risk for the ADHD child, sometimes finds itself quietly more alone than it was before the diagnosis. Naming this pattern, and actively counteracting it with relationships and communities that offer understanding without judgment, is a practical act of self-preservation for the family as a whole.

One dimension of family stress that is rarely named in parenting conversations is the phenomenon of secondary shame. Parents of children with ADHD frequently internalize the cultural message that their child's behavior reflects their parenting. When the child has a public meltdown, when the teacher sends home another note, when a playdate ends early, the parent does not only manage the child's behavior. She manages her own internal narrative about what that behavior means about her. This secondary shame, layered on top of the daily management demands, is an additional burden that exhausts without being visible and that interferes with the parent's capacity to respond clearly in the moment.

Recognizing secondary shame as a feature of the ADHD parenting experience, rather than a personal failing, is the first step toward reducing its influence. The behavior is not about your competence. It is about a neurological condition that produces behavior that is difficult to manage in public environments. These are different statements, and living inside the correct one makes a measurable difference in how much cognitive and emotional resource is available for the actual work of parenting.

The normalizing frame that is most useful here is this: the challenges in your household are not evidence that you are doing something wrong. They are the predictable consequences of a genuine neurological condition that creates genuine difficulty in the environments where children live. Other families in your situation face the same challenges. The ones who navigate them with the least damage are not the ones with fewer difficulties. They are the ones who have the most accurate picture of what they are dealing with and the most realistic set of expectations about what support looks like.

Managing Sibling Conflict and Resentment

The sibling of a child with ADHD occupies one of the most complicated positions in the family. She is not the child who needs the most help, which means she receives less of it. She is not the child whose behavior requires the most management, which means her needs get pushed to later. She is the child who has learned, often early, that the fastest way to receive parental attention is to be in crisis, and she has often concluded, correctly, that the threshold for her crises to be taken seriously is higher than the threshold for her brother's.

This is not intentional parental neglect. It is the predictable result of a household where one child's needs are urgent and visible and another's are less so. The sibling who is doing reasonably well, who is not generating behavioral incidents, who is managing school and friendships without apparent difficulty, is a child who makes it easy to direct attention elsewhere. She knows this, and she feels it, even if she does not say so.

The dynamic that develops most reliably in siblings of children with ADHD involves some combination of resentment and compensation. Resentment at the asymmetry of attention and rules: why does he get screen time even when he did not finish his homework? Why do we leave restaurants early because of him? Why do I have to be quiet during his homework time? Compensation in the form of behavior that is more reliable, more cooperative, and more manageable than the sibling's, often motivated by an implicit understanding that the household cannot handle two children who need significant management simultaneously. This compensating behavior can look like maturity and is sometimes praised as such.

What it sometimes is, is a child suppressing her own needs in order to reduce the overall pressure in the system.

The equity principle that resolves this most effectively is not equal treatment but appropriate treatment. Equal treatment is impossible when children have different needs, and attempting it creates resentment in both directions. The ADHD child resents accommodations being withdrawn in the name of fairness. The sibling resents accommodations being extended in the name of fairness. The more productive conversation, conducted with age-appropriate honesty, is: "We give everyone in this family what they need. You both need different things. Here is what each of you gets, and here is why." Most children can accept difference when it is explained with respect for their intelligence rather than defended as a rule.

There is also a specific conversation worth having with the sibling about her brother's diagnosis that many parents avoid for fear of saying the wrong thing. Children who live with a sibling with ADHD generally know that something is different about him long before they have language for it. Giving the sibling accurate, age-appropriate information about ADHD, framed not as an explanation for behavior she must simply accept but as information that helps her understand what she is living with, gives her something more useful than the story she is likely constructing on her own. "His brain works differently and sometimes makes it hard for him to control his impulses. That is not an excuse, and it is not your fault, and you are still allowed to tell us when something is unfair." That framing holds the child accountable while giving the sibling a framework that is more accurate and more useful than "he just does that.

Dedicated one-on-one time with the sibling, specifically protected from any discussion of the ADHD child or his challenges, communicates directly that she is seen as a complete person and not only as a member of a household organized around her brother. This does not require elaborate planning. It requires that the time exists, that it is consistent, and that during it you are genuinely present with her, not mentally running through the management tasks waiting for you when it ends.

Keeping Your Relationship With Your Partner Strong

The couple relationship in an ADHD household is under pressures that most parenting books do not adequately address. The relentless daily demand of managing a child with ADHD depletes the energy that a relationship requires. The divergences in parenting approach that exist in every couple are magnified when the stakes are higher and the child's responses to those approaches are more immediate and more visible. The conversations that sustain a couple's connection, the ones that are not about logistics or children or problems to be solved, become increasingly rare when the household is in a sustained high-demand period.

The divergence in parenting approach is worth examining specifically because it is a common source of conflict that couples often do not know how to address without one partner feeling criticized. One parent tends toward more structure, earlier consequences, clearer limits. The other tends toward more flexibility, more emotional attunement, less immediate enforcement. In a typical household, these differences exist in productive tension. In an ADHD household, they become visible and contested more frequently because the decisions are higher-stakes and the results of different approaches are immediately observable. The parent who implements a consequence sees the child's reaction. The parent who offers understanding sees a different child reaction. Each concludes that their approach is working better.

The most functional approach to parenting disagreements in this context is not to resolve them to a single method but to build a coherent enough shared framework that the child receives a consistent signal even when the specific implementation varies. Two parents who both agree that predictability, skill-building, and the relationship with the child are the priorities can disagree significantly on specific tactics and still produce a consistent environment for the child. Two parents who have never discussed their underlying approach are likely to undermine each other in ways that the child learns to exploit and that generate conflict between the adults.

The couple's relationship also requires the same deliberate investment that every other important relationship in the household requires. The insight from Chapter 12 about the emotional bank account applies here too: the relationship sustains difficulty better when it has been actively maintained rather than left to run on whatever energy remains after the children are managed. This does not require elaborate effort. It requires a regular, intentional practice of connection that is protected from the management demands of the household: a conversation that is not about logistics, a shared activity that is genuinely enjoyable, an acknowledgment of what the other person is carrying that goes beyond the transactional. Small, consistent investments in the couple relationship do more for its resilience than occasional large ones.

There is a specific risk in ADHD households that is worth naming directly: the risk that the parenting identity becomes the primary identity for both partners, particularly during the years when the child's needs are most demanding. When all of the couple's shared attention, shared problem-solving, and shared emotional investment goes toward the child's challenges, the couple's shared identity gradually narrows to the point where they are co-managers of a household with a complex child and not much else. This narrowing is rarely chosen. It happens incrementally, through a series of small decisions to prioritize the child's needs over the couple's, each of which is reasonable in isolation and cumulatively corrosive.

The couples who navigate this most effectively do not find more time. They protect the time they have with the same intentionality they bring to other non-negotiable family commitments. A weekly hour that belongs to the couple, not to logistics, not to problem-solving about the child, not to the accumulated to-do list of family management, is an investment in the structure that everything else in the family depends on. It does not solve the stress. It maintains the relationship that carries the stress, which amounts to the same thing.

When Extended Family Does Not Understand ADHD

The grandparent who thinks it is a discipline problem. The uncle who says he was exactly like that as a kid and no one made a fuss. The aunt who asks whether you have considered reducing sugar. These responses are common, and they are wearing, and they arrive most reliably at family gatherings where you are already managing a high-stimulation environment with a child who is at his most dysregulated.

The first decision to make about extended family is a strategic one: who is worth educating, and who is not? This is not a cynical calculation. It is a practical one. Educating someone about ADHD requires time, emotional investment, and a willingness on their part to update their understanding. For family members who interact frequently with your son, who have a meaningful relationship with him, and who show some genuine openness to understanding, the investment is worth making. For family members who are encountered twice a year and who have demonstrated consistent resistance to information that contradicts their existing framework, the investment is likely to produce frustration rather than understanding.

For the family members who are worth educating, the approach that works most reliably is the same one that works with teachers: specific, concrete, behavioral, and forward-looking. Not a lecture on neuroscience, but a specific observation: "He does much better when we give him a heads-up before we leave, not when we announce it abruptly. If you could help us with that today, it would make a significant difference." This invites participation, not diagnosis delivery. It gives the family member something concrete to do: a specific behavior, not a belief to update, which is a much lower bar.

For the comments and judgments that arrive regardless, the most sustainable response is often the shortest one. "We're working on it" closes a conversation without creating conflict. "I hear you" acknowledges the statement without endorsing it. The conversations you choose not to have conserve energy for the ones that matter. Protecting your son from comments that undermine his self-concept is a priority; protecting yourself from a conversation that will not change anything is equally legitimate.

There is a particular challenge that arises at family gatherings specifically: the child with ADHD in a high-stimulation environment with reduced structure and unpredictable social demands, surrounded by adults who are watching him more carefully than they watch other children, and who will interpret any behavioral difficulty as confirmation of whatever they already believe. This is a difficult combination, and the parent who walks into it with no strategy is likely to spend the gathering in a state of elevated vigilance that transmits directly to the child.

Practical strategies that reduce this pressure include pre-briefing the child about what to expect from the event: who will be there, how long it will last, what the plan is when he needs a break, and what the exit signal is if things become too much. These are the same predictability tools from Chapter 8 applied to a different context. They work for the same reason. A child who knows what to expect from the event requires significantly less regulatory energy to manage the novelty than a child who is encountering it fresh.

Establishing a physical exit point, a specific room or outdoor space where the child can decompress away from the social stimulation when he needs to, serves both the child and the gathering. The child who can leave the table when he is overwhelmed and return when he is regulated is less likely to have a behavioral incident that becomes the story everyone discusses afterward. The space does not advertise his difficulty. It manages it, quietly and effectively, without drawing the attention of every family member who is already watching.

One practical point about grandparents specifically: the grandparents who are willing to learn, even imperfectly, even with outdated terminology, are a resource worth cultivating. A grandparent who understands that the child needs a heads-up before transitions, who knows that hunger and tiredness amplify his dysregulation, and who has learned to engage him one-on-one in smaller settings has become a genuine support, not an additional management challenge. The investment in that particular family member's understanding produces returns that can span years.

Creating Family Rituals That Work for Everyone

The distinction between a routine and a ritual is worth naming clearly. A routine is a sequence of actions performed to accomplish something: getting everyone out of the door in the morning, completing homework, going through the bedtime sequence. A ritual is a repeated shared experience that generates meaning beyond its functional purpose. A family that has only routines has efficiency. A family that also has rituals has identity.

Children with ADHD benefit from rituals for the same reason they benefit from routines: predictability creates safety, and knowing what to expect reduces the cognitive load of managing novelty. But the benefit of rituals goes beyond that. A family ritual communicates, through repetition, that we do this because we are the kind of family that does this. It generates a sense of belonging that is not contingent on any particular day's behavior and that persists through the weeks when everything has been difficult.

The rituals that work best for ADHD households share certain characteristics. They are short enough to be completed without losing the child's engagement. They are sensory and experiential enough to hold attention in a way that abstract or verbal activities do not. They are repeatable in consistent form rather than improvised each time, because the repetition is what builds the meaning. And they are genuinely inclusive of all the children in the family, not structured around the ADHD child's needs to the exclusion of the sibling's.

Specific examples that meet these criteria: a Sunday morning breakfast where everyone contributes one thing they are looking forward to in the week ahead; a

Friday evening walk or drive that functions as a physical transition between the school week and the weekend; a nightly check-in at bedtime that is brief, consistent, and private between parent and each child; an annual family tradition tied to a season or holiday that centers on doing something together, not on receiving something. None of these requires significant resources or elaborate planning. Each of them, repeated consistently over months and years, builds something that cannot be generated any other way.

The qualifier that matters most for ADHD families is realistic. A ritual that requires conditions that are difficult to reliably produce (a quiet dinner with sustained conversation, extended focused participation, seamless cooperation between siblings) will fail often enough that it becomes a source of disappointment, not connection. A ritual that works given the actual family you have, with its actual energy levels and its actual dynamics, will build something genuine. Imperfect rituals that happen are worth more than ideal rituals that do not.

The rituals that serve the sibling, not only the ADHD child, deserve specific attention. A family that has designed its rituals primarily around what works for the ADHD child has, unintentionally, continued the pattern of organizing the family around one member's needs. The most effective family rituals are ones that have something genuinely appealing for each person in the family, not just the one with the most complex requirements. The sibling who looks forward to Sunday breakfast because she gets to choose the music is participating fully, not accommodating her brother. That distinction matters for her sense of belonging in the family.

The longer-term function of family rituals is the one that is hardest to see while you are in the middle of building them. Over years, they accumulate into a shared family narrative: these are the things we do, and doing them together is part of what makes us who we are. For a child with ADHD who may struggle to sustain a coherent sense of himself across different contexts and different days, being embedded in a family with a consistent and recognizable shared life is a source of continuity and stability that no intervention provides directly. The family narrative that the rituals build is not a treatment. It is a context in which the treatment can work better, because the child who knows where he belongs is a child with more internal resources available for everything else.

Rituals also provide a reliable source of positive shared experience in households where the daily interaction between family members is often organized around management and correction. A family that eats dinner together with reliable frequency, that has a Friday evening practice that everyone participates in, that marks the beginning and end of the school week with something consistent, is generating positive shared memories at a rate that changes the texture of how family members experience each other. The sibling who associates home primarily with difficulty has a different family experience than the sibling who associates home with difficulty and also with the things they do together that feel like belonging.

Chapter 19: Taking Care of Yourself While You Take Care of Him

You cannot pour from an empty cup.

This is the chapter you read last, if you read it at all. Not because it is less important than the others, but because it is the chapter that feels least urgent. There is always something else that needs your attention first: the homework that is not done, the email from the teacher, the medication appointment, the IEP meeting, the sibling who has been waiting for you all afternoon. By the time you get to yourself, there is nothing left to get to.

That pattern is the problem this chapter addresses. Not by asking you to carve out spa weekends or practice elaborate self-care rituals you do not have time for. By making a simpler case: your capacity to be present for your son, to regulate your own responses, to make clear decisions under pressure, and to maintain the relationship that all of the other strategies in this book depend on, is not separate from your wellbeing. It is a direct product of it. Taking care of yourself is not indulgence. It is the maintenance of the infrastructure that everything else runs on.

The Cost of Chronic Stress That Parents Rarely Talk About

There is a body of research on parenting stress in ADHD households that most parents never encounter, because it is published in clinical journals read by clinicians and not by the people whose lives it describes. The consistent finding across multiple studies is that parents of children with ADHD report significantly higher levels of stress, anxiety, and depression than parents of neurotypical children. These are not marginal differences. They are substantial and persistent, and they correlate with the severity of the child's symptoms and the chronicity of the parenting demands.

What chronic stress does to a parent's functioning is something that affects every interaction she has with her child, and it operates through mechanisms that are specific and worth understanding. The first is emotional regulation capacity. The prefrontal cortex, which is responsible for inhibiting reactive responses and choosing deliberate ones, functions less effectively under sustained stress. A parent who is chronically depleted does not have the same access to her regulatory capacity as a parent who is not. She is more reactive, more easily triggered, and less able to pause before responding in the moments when pausing most matters. This is not a character flaw. It is the predictable consequence of a system operating beyond its sustainable load.

The second mechanism is cognitive bandwidth. Parenting a child with ADHD requires significant cognitive resources: tracking medication schedules, holding the child's behavioral patterns in mind well enough to anticipate problems before they occur, managing communications with multiple professionals and school staff, making real-time decisions in difficult situations. Chronic stress degrades the quality of this cognitive work in ways that are measurable. Sustained cortisol elevation, the physiological marker of chronic stress, impairs working memory and decision-making. A parent under chronic stress is making parenting decisions with a compromised cognitive toolkit, and she often does not know it because the degradation is gradual and she has no point of comparison.

The third consequence is physical. Chronic stress produces physical health consequences that accumulate over months and years: disrupted sleep, suppressed immune function, elevated cardiovascular risk, chronic pain. These consequences are not hypothetical. They are documented and they are reversible when the stress is addressed, but they compound when it is not.

Parental burnout is a recognized clinical construct, distinct from general burnout or depression, that describes a specific state of exhaustion that results from the sustained demands of parenting with inadequate resources. It involves emotional exhaustion from the parenting role, a sense of distance or emotional detachment from the child, a loss of the parenting satisfaction and competence that the parent previously experienced, and a sense of being trapped in a role from which there is no exit. Parents of children with complex needs are at elevated risk. Recognizing parental burnout as a real condition with real consequences, not as weakness or inadequate commitment, is the first step toward addressing it.

There is a specific pattern in ADHD parenting households worth naming: the asymmetry between the parent's internal experience and what is visible externally. Many parents of children with ADHD present as functionally capable, managing school communications and appointments and behavioral strategies with apparent competence, while carrying a level of internal depletion that has no outlet. The gap between what is visible and what is actually happening internally is itself a source of stress, because it means the parent is managing both the demands and the appearance of managing the demands. Giving herself permission to acknowledge the gap, at minimum internally and ideally in at least one relationship where honesty is safe, is not a descent into self-pity. It is an accurate accounting of what she is actually carrying.

The normalizing statement that belongs here is direct: you are not struggling because you are not trying hard enough. You are struggling because you are doing one of the most demanding jobs there is, with fewer external supports than the job requires, in a cultural context that often frames parenting difficulty as personal failure. The exhaustion is proportionate to the demand. Treating yourself with the same interpretive generosity you are learning to apply to your son is not self-indulgence. It is accuracy.

Managing Guilt, Frustration, and the Urge to Fix Everything

The guilt that parents of children with ADHD carry is persistent and specific. It is not the general parental guilt of wondering whether you are doing enough. It is the more acute guilt of having lost your patience with a child who is already struggling, of having said something sharp in a moment of exhaustion that you immediately regretted, of having calculated that you do not have enough left to be present in the way the situation calls for and choosing to manage rather than connect. This guilt is painful, and it is also, paradoxically, a sign of caring deeply. A parent who did not care would not feel it.

The problem with guilt is not that it exists but that most parents respond to it with self-punishment: replaying the moment repeatedly, cataloguing what they should have done differently, carrying the weight of it forward into the next interaction with the child. Self-punishment does not produce better parenting. It depletes the resources that better parenting requires and maintains a state of internal preoccupation that reduces the parent's capacity to be present. The parent who cannot forgive herself for yesterday's loss of patience is running yesterday's interaction in the background during today's, which reduces the cognitive and emotional bandwidth available for today.

Self-compassion is not a therapeutic luxury or a form of letting yourself off the hook. It is a cognitive skill with measurable effects on performance and resilience. The research on self-compassion in caregiving contexts consistently finds that caregivers who can apply the same interpretive generosity to themselves that they apply to others maintain their functioning longer, recover from failures faster, and report higher quality of care provision. The self-compassionate parent is not the parent who excuses poor behavior. She is the parent who acknowledges what happened, understands why it happened without catastrophizing it, and returns to the task with her resources intact.

Frustration is the other emotion that deserves direct acknowledgment. The frustration of implementing a strategy consistently and seeing no measurable change. The frustration of a conversation with a teacher that ends exactly where it began. The frustration of a day where every transition was a battle and every meal was a negotiation and the child went to bed having done none of the things that needed to happen. This frustration is not evidence of insufficient love. It is the normal emotional response to sustained effort that produces inconsistent results, which is exactly what parenting an ADHD child involves.

The urge to fix everything is worth addressing as a specific trap. Parents of children with ADHD often develop a vigilance about the child's environment that expands over time, until they are managing not just the immediate situation but trying to anticipate and prevent every possible difficulty two or three steps ahead. This vigilance has a real cost: it is exhausting, it is often ineffective because many difficulties cannot be anticipated, and it prevents the child from developing his own capacity to navigate difficulty because the parent is always there first. Reducing the urge to fix does not mean reducing care. It means directing energy toward what you can actually influence and releasing the rest.

There is a practical distinction that helps with this: the difference between problems you can solve today, problems you can influence over time, and problems you cannot influence at all. The child's neurological wiring is in the third category. The quality of today's homework session is in the first. The trajectory of his academic confidence over the next two years is in the second. A parent who is spending significant energy on the third category, trying to will away or worry away the fundamental nature of the child's brain, is depleting herself in ways that produce no return. Releasing the third category is not giving up. It is redirecting toward where effort actually matters.

Building a Support System That Actually Helps

The isolation that many parents of children with ADHD experience is compounded by a specific social dynamic: the people in their lives who are not parenting a child with ADHD genuinely cannot understand what the experience is like from the inside. They offer advice that reflects a different parenting experience. They suggest solutions that would work for neurotypical children and do not work for this one. They express a confidence in outcomes ("he'll be fine, kids grow out of these things") that the parent inside the experience does not share. Their support is well-intentioned and often feels worse than no support, because it underscores the gap between their understanding and the reality.

The most useful form of support comes from people who share the same or similar experience. Parent support groups for ADHD, whether local or online, provide a social context in which the specifics of the experience are understood without explanation. The parent who says "he melted down for forty minutes over the pencil not being sharpened enough" does not need to justify the scale of that event to a room of people who have experienced the same. The shared understanding produces a form of relief that is qualitatively different from the sympathy of someone who is trying to understand from outside. Finding this community, whether through a local CHADD chapter, an online forum, or a school-based parent group, is an investment in your own sustainability that pays returns disproportionate to the effort it takes.

Individual therapy is a resource worth considering not because there is something wrong with you but because parenting a child with complex needs generates its own psychological material that benefits from a dedicated space to process. The grief that Chapter 18 named, the secondary shame, the guilt, the frustration, the relationship with your own history that parenting activates, are all things that accumulate and that do not resolve through time alone. A therapist who has experience with parents of children with disabilities or neurodevelopmental conditions is particularly useful, because she brings a framework for the specific experience you are navigating.

The request for help is where many parents get stuck, because asking for help feels like admitting that you cannot manage what you are supposed to manage. The reframe that is most accurate is: you are managing something that requires more support than any single person reasonably has. Asking for a break from a trusted family member or friend, finding a babysitter who can handle your son's specific needs so you can have two hours that are not organized around him, outsourcing one of the logistical tasks that is consuming your cognitive load, are all acts of household management, not admissions of failure.

There is also a category of support that is specific to ADHD parenting and that is worth seeking out explicitly: professionals who understand ADHD and who can speak to your situation with relevant knowledge. A pediatrician who dismisses your concerns about behavior, a therapist who has no framework for executive function deficits, a school counselor who has not worked with ADHD students, are not useful support even with the best intentions. Actively seeking clinicians and educators who have relevant experience with your son's profile, rather than defaulting to whoever is available, is an investment in the quality of guidance you receive that has downstream effects on the quality of the parenting decisions you make.

Distinguishing useful support from support that depletes is also a practical skill. Advice from someone who does not understand ADHD and who frames it as a parenting problem is not support. A family member who judges your choices while nominally helping is not support. The help that actually helps is the help that reduces your load without adding commentary about how the load should be carried.

How to Stay Present When You Are Depleted

The moments when presence is hardest are the moments when presence matters most. A child who is dysregulated needs a regulated adult. A child who is heading toward a meltdown needs someone whose nervous system can serve as a stabilizing anchor. And those are exactly the moments when the parent who is depleted, who has already managed six difficult transitions and one school phone call and a homework battle, is least equipped to provide what is needed.

The first practical tool for depleted presence is recognizing the depletion before it produces an outcome you regret. This requires developing a personal early warning system: the specific internal signals that tell you, before you are fully dysregulated, that you are close to your limit. For some parents it is a physical sensation, tension in the shoulders or a shortness of breath. For others it is a quality of thought, a narrowing of perspective that makes every small obstacle feel like a large one. For others it is emotional, a specific irritability that is disproportionate to the trigger.

Whatever your early signal is, it is more actionable than the recognition that comes after you have already responded in a way you wish you had not.

When you identify the depletion signal early, the most effective intervention is brief and physiological: slow, intentional breathing with an extended exhale activates the parasympathetic nervous system and reduces the acute stress response within minutes. Stepping outside for sixty seconds, splashing cold water on the face, making brief physical contact with the environment through hands or feet, are all fast physiological resets that are available in any setting without requiring preparation or explanation. None of these is a solution to chronic depletion. Each of them creates a small window of regulatory capacity that can change the quality of the next interaction.

The distinction between full presence and good-enough presence is one that depleted parents need permission to make. Full presence, the state of being completely attentive and emotionally available and responsive with your whole self, is not available at the end of a hard day. Good-enough presence, the state of being physically there, making eye contact, responding instead of withdrawing, is available most of the time and is what the child needs most of the time. Saving full presence for the moments that most require it, for the repair conversation, for the child-led play session, for the specific connection moment you have prioritized, while accepting good-enough presence in the intervals, is not a compromise. It is resource management.

There is a specific risk in the depleted parent's relationship with her own internal states: the tendency to suppress awareness of depletion in order to continue functioning. A parent who has learned to override her own signals, because the demands do not pause when she is tired, gradually loses the ability to read those signals accurately. The early warning system becomes unreliable because it has been ignored often enough that the signals do not register until they are acute. Rebuilding that awareness requires deliberate attention to internal states, not as a therapeutic exercise but as a practical monitoring practice: how am I doing right now, and what does that mean for how I approach the next hour? This question, asked honestly a few times per day, costs almost nothing and changes the quality of the decisions that follow.

Small regenerative pauses built into the day, not grand self-care gestures but two-minute investments in something that refuels rather than depletes, matter more cumulatively than their size suggests. A cup of coffee made and drunk without a screen. Five minutes of walking outside between the school pickup and the homework hour. A brief conversation with an adult who is not about managing anything. These micro-recoveries do not eliminate depletion. They slow the rate at which it accumulates, which changes what is available at the end of the day.

What Good Parenting Looks Like on Hard Days

The definition of a successful parenting day that most parents carry is not explicit, but it is real and it is usually something like: everyone got where they needed to go, the homework got done, no one melted down at a level that required serious intervention, and no one went to bed angry or crying. By this definition, bad days are frequent and good days are the exception. By this definition, many parents of children with ADHD are failing most of the time.

A more accurate and more useful definition of parenting success on a hard day is narrower and more achievable: you held the relationship at the center even when the day was difficult. You did not let the difficulty of the behavior erode your fundamental commitment to the child. You repaired what needed repairing, even imperfectly. You were present enough, often enough, that the child went to bed knowing that the relationship between you is stable, regardless of how today went.

This is the "good enough" standard of parenting that the developmental psychologist Donald Winnicott described in a different era with different language, and that the research since has consistently supported. Children do not need perfect parenting. They need parenting that is reliably warm, that repairs ruptures consistently, and that communicates a secure underlying relationship even when individual interactions are difficult. The standard is achievable. A parent who loses patience and then repairs, who has a hard day and then comes back the next day, who is inconsistent in her implementation and consistent in her love, is providing what developmental research identifies as what children need.

The specific distortion that perfectionism introduces in ADHD parenting is a tendency to evaluate the parenting by the worst moment of the day rather than by the whole of it. The parent who managed eight difficult situations well and lost patience in the ninth focuses on the ninth. The parent who spent two hours navigating a difficult homework session with more patience than she knew she had and then snapped at dinner carries the snap to bed. This accounting system consistently undervalues what was actually done and consistently overweights the failures, producing a self-assessment that is systematically more negative than the reality.

The repair that happens after a hard moment is worth naming explicitly as a parenting act, not a correction of a parenting failure. When you come back to your son after losing patience, when you name what happened and take responsibility for your part of it, when you make the repair without over-explaining or collapsing into excessive apology, you are demonstrating something that will serve him for the rest of his life: that it is possible to have a rupture in an important relationship and to come back from it with the relationship intact. That demonstration is not a consolation for the hard moment. It is a distinct and valuable thing that the hard moment made possible.

Hard days do not cancel good ones. The record is cumulative and it belongs to the whole arc of the relationship, not to any single day within it. A child who has a parent who shows up consistently, who repairs consistently, who communicates consistently that the relationship is more important than any individual incident, is building a secure attachment that a single bad day cannot erode. The moments of genuine connection that happen within hard days, the moment when you caught each other's eye at the dinner table and both started laughing despite everything, the moment when he came to you after his meltdown was over and let you hold him, are not footnotes to the difficulty. They are the thing itself.

Redefining what a good parenting day looks like is not lowering the standard. It is replacing a standard that was never accurate with one that reflects what developmental research actually identifies as what children need. The parent who holds this revised standard, who evaluates her day by whether the relationship was maintained and repaired, who counts the moments of genuine connection as evidence of success, is working from a framework that produces more accurate self-assessment, more sustainable effort, and more of the quality of presence that her son actually benefits from. The perfectionist standard produces guilt that depletes. The accurate standard produces a foundation that holds.

Chapter 20: The Long Game

The days are long, but the years are short.

Parents who are in the early years of raising a son with ADHD cannot yet see what parents who are five or ten years further along already know: the picture changes more than you expect, in ways you cannot fully predict, and the work you do now matters in ways you will not always be able to trace directly. The child who is eight is not the child who will be thirteen, and the child who is thirteen is not the man who will be twenty-three. What you are building is not a solution to this year's problems. It is a foundation that will hold across versions of your son you have not yet met.

This chapter is about the long view. Not the optimistic version that minimizes the difficulty, or the catastrophic version that projects today's worst day forward indefinitely. The honest version: what this journey actually looks like across time, what is realistic to expect at each stage, and what the work of today is building toward.

What Raising an ADHD Boy Looks Like at Each Stage

The trajectory of ADHD across development is not a straight line, and understanding that fact before you encounter the discontinuities makes them significantly less disorienting when they arrive. ADHD is a developmental condition, meaning its expression changes as the brain matures and as the demands of the environment change. The child you are parenting today is operating inside a specific developmental window with specific challenges that are real but not permanent. The window will shift.

In the preschool and early elementary years, the challenges are primarily behavioral and regulatory: the child who cannot sit still, who disrupts the classroom, who melts down over transitions, who is already being described as a problem before he fully understands that there is a problem. The intervention work at this stage is environmental and relational: reducing unnecessary friction, building routines, establishing the parent-child connection that will be the platform for everything else. The preschool child with ADHD is not yet old enough to understand his own brain or to participate meaningfully in managing it. He is old enough to know whether the adults around him are a source of safety or a source of pressure.

The elementary years are when academic demands meet executive function deficits head-on, and the gap between what the child is capable of knowing and what he can produce on paper becomes visible in ways that generate both school difficulty and shame. This is often the period when the diagnosis arrives, when medication is first discussed, and when parents begin the education in systems, accommodations, and advocacy that this book has addressed. The elementary child is also old enough to begin understanding something about his own brain, to learn that different people think differently, and to start building the self-awareness that will serve him later.

The transition to middle school is the discontinuity that surprises parents most reliably. A child who had found some equilibrium in elementary school, who had a known teacher, a familiar environment, and an established set of accommodations, suddenly faces multiple teachers who do not know him, a larger and more complex social environment, organizational demands that are significantly greater, and a peer culture that has become more socially consequential. Regressions at this transition are not failures. They are predictable responses to a genuinely more demanding environment, and they should be anticipated and planned for rather than treated as evidence that earlier progress has been lost.

One of the most important reframes available to parents in the elementary years is this: understanding that the behavioral and academic difficulties they are managing are not simply the permanent features of who their son is. They are the current expression of a neurological profile in a specific developmental context. That context changes. The middle school student who is organized around peer relationships and who finds his dysregulation is less tolerated in the more complex social environment of those years is not the same person as the elementary student who simply could not sit still. The high school student who begins to find his academic footing when a subject genuinely interests him is not the same student who failed to turn in sixth grade homework. These are different versions of the same person at different developmental stages, and conflating them, treating the ten-year-old's difficulties as the inevitable adult's outcome, is one of the most common and most damaging mistakes parents make.

High school brings the added complexity of identity formation in a context where the ADHD student may be comparing himself to peers whose academic trajectory looks very different from his. It also brings the beginning of what Chapter 20.4 addresses more fully: the gradual transfer of self-management responsibility from parent to adolescent. The high school years are the training ground for adult autonomy, and the parents who navigate them most effectively are the ones who have been building toward that transfer for years, releasing control incrementally as competence develops, not maintaining management and then dropping it at eighteen.

Preparing Your Son for Adolescence and the Challenges Ahead

Adolescence intensifies everything. The hormonal changes of puberty amplify the impulsivity that is already one of ADHD's core features. The social complexity of middle and high school increases the consequences of impulsive decisions in ways that were not true in elementary school. The identity construction that is the psychological work of adolescence happens in a child whose sense of self may already be complicated by years of difficulty and the accumulated feedback described in Chapter 17. And the risk behaviors that adolescence makes available, substances, reckless choices, social situations with significant consequences, are more accessible and more appealing to a brain that is driven by novelty and reward.

Preparation for adolescence is not the same as prevention of the worst outcomes, although it does reduce risk. It is the construction of the internal architecture that allows a teenager to navigate difficulty without the parent's presence: self-awareness, the ability to recognize his own state and its causes; self-regulation skills, imperfect but available; the capacity to ask for help when he is in over his head; and a relationship with at least one trusted adult, ideally but not necessarily a parent, that provides a reliable point of return when things go wrong.

The transfer of responsibility from parent to teenager requires being deliberate and gradual. A parent who has managed every dimension of the child's life through elementary school and hands it all over at thirteen is not teaching autonomy. She is creating a situation where the teenager has neither the skills nor the practice to manage what has been given to him. The parent who has been incrementally handing pieces of responsibility across the elementary years, who has been asking "what do you think you should do?" before providing the answer, who has allowed natural consequences to teach when they were safe enough to allow, is preparing a teenager who has some experience managing himself.

There is a specific developmental paradox in ADHD adolescence worth naming: the teenager who needs more parental guidance is also the teenager who is most motivated to reject it. Adolescence, for all teenagers, involves a psychological move toward autonomy and away from parental authority. For the ADHD teenager, whose impulse control is still developing and whose decision-making in high-stakes social situations is genuinely risky, the timing of this developmental push creates a particular challenge. He needs more scaffolding than his neurotypical peers at the exact moment when he is most resistant to receiving it.

The parents who navigate this most effectively have shifted from direct management to consultative support before the adolescent years make direct management untenable. They have been asking their son's opinion, offering choices, explaining reasoning, and building his sense of competence across the elementary years so that by thirteen, the relationship is already structured around his growing agency. The transition to adolescent autonomy is smoother when it is the continuation of an existing direction.

The relationship between parent and adolescent is the variable that research most consistently identifies as protective for ADHD teenagers. Not the strictness of the rules, not the quality of the medication management, not the sophistication of the school accommodations. The quality of the connection between parent and child, established during the elementary years through the kind of work described throughout this book, is what allows an adolescent who is struggling to tell a parent what is actually happening rather than managing it alone. That relationship is built long before adolescence, in the small daily deposits described in Chapter 12, in the repairs after hard days, in the consistent message that the relationship is more important than any individual behavior. A teenager who has that foundation does not need his parent to manage every decision. He needs to know that when he makes a genuinely bad one, the conversation he has to have afterward will not end the relationship.

What Success Looks Like for a Boy With ADHD

The educational system measures success through a specific and narrow set of metrics: grades, test scores, behavior in structured settings, compliance with adult expectations. These metrics are not irrelevant. They have consequences for access and opportunity that are real. But they are also deeply misaligned with the strengths of the ADHD brain, and a child who is evaluated primarily through them will almost inevitably come up short in ways that do not reflect his actual capacities or his eventual possibilities.

Adults with ADHD who have built lives that work for them share certain characteristics that are worth naming, because they are different from the characteristics that school metrics identify. They found environments where their particular profile was an asset rather than a liability. The surgeon who thrives in the high-stakes, fast-decision, procedural environment of an operating room. The entrepreneur whose ability to hold multiple threads simultaneously and to generate ideas at a pace that would overwhelm a more inhibited mind is exactly what the role requires. The journalist, the chef, the engineer, the coach, the artist, the first responder: the roles that reward the cognitive profile of ADHD are numerous and varied, and most of them are not accurately predicted by middle school GPA.

What these adults also share is some version of self-knowledge: an understanding of how they work best, what environments support them and which ones undermine them, and enough self-advocacy capacity to seek and arrange the conditions they need. The teenager who knows that he cannot write a term paper in a single sitting but can produce good work in four ninety-minute sessions across a week is more likely to succeed than the teenager who has been told to "just sit down and do it" and has never been helped to understand what actually works for his brain.

The parent's long-term job is not to engineer the child's success in a conventional sense. It is to help him develop the self-knowledge and the flexibility to find his own path. That means exposing him to a range of environments and activities, not only the ones that school rewards. It means naming what you observe about how he works, what engages him, where his energy goes naturally. It means being genuinely curious about who he is becoming, not only concerned about whether he is meeting the benchmarks his peers are meeting. A child who is raised with genuine curiosity about who he is develops a different relationship with himself than a child who is raised primarily inside the frame of what is wrong with him.

There is a longer-term economic reality worth stating directly: the adult labor market has changed in ways that are favorable to the ADHD profile. The rise of entrepreneurship, the expansion of creative industries, the premium placed on adaptability and the ability to synthesize information quickly and take risks that more inhibited temperaments avoid, has produced environments where the

ADHD cognitive profile is genuinely competitive. The student who graduates high school with a C average but who has developed real expertise in something he cares about, who can solve problems under pressure and generate ideas faster than he can implement them, is not at a disadvantage in a landscape that rewards those qualities. He is at a disadvantage specifically in the pathway from high GPA to selective university to credential-based career, and there are other pathways.

This is not an argument for accepting academic underperformance. It is an argument for holding the child's trajectory lightly enough that you do not mistake the road he is currently on for the only one available to him. The map of possible paths is wider than what is visible from inside the school system at thirteen, and a parent who keeps that wider view available to both of them gives her son something genuinely useful.

Teaching Your Son to Understand and Advocate for Himself

The most important long-term outcome of the work described in this book is not that your son will have better grades or fewer meltdowns or a more organized backpack. It is that he will be able to function in the world without you managing it for him. That requires a specific kind of knowledge: knowledge of himself, how his brain works, what helps him and what hinders him, and the language to communicate that to others.

Self-advocacy is a skill that is built over years, not installed at a single age. It begins with the parent naming what she observes: "I notice you do your best thinking when you can move around" or "it seems like you need a few minutes to transition before you can engage with the new thing." These observations, offered consistently and without judgment across years, give the child a vocabulary for his own experience before he has developed it on his own. By adolescence, the goal is for him to have enough self-knowledge to be able to say to a teacher, an employer, or a collaborator: "I work best when I can break large tasks into smaller ones with deadlines for each piece" or "I need to take notes in my own format, not the one on the board, because my visual processing works differently."

This is not a demand for accommodation as a right, though the right exists. It is the capacity to participate in designing his own working conditions, which is what successful adults with ADHD do regardless of whether they have formal accommodations available to them. A man who knows he cannot reliably hold verbal instructions past the third item and who has developed the habit of writing things down immediately is managing his own neurology. He does not need anyone to do it for him. He needs to have learned that this is what works.

The conversation about ADHD that begins in the elementary years, when a parent explains in age-appropriate terms why his brain works differently, continues across adolescence in more sophisticated forms. A teenager can understand neuroscience in more detail. He can understand the research on what helps ADHD brains, and he can begin to apply it to his own choices: about sleep, about study conditions, about how he organizes his time, about the situations where he knows he is at risk of making decisions he will regret. This progressive building of self-knowledge is the work that continues long after the strategies in this book are no longer the right size for the version of your son who exists then.

There is a practical dimension to self-advocacy worth addressing specifically: the adult systems your son will eventually navigate, university disability services, workplace accommodations, healthcare management, all require him to articulate his needs clearly and to self-identify proactively. Many adults with ADHD who received support throughout their school years arrive at university and do not access disability services because they have never been taught to identify themselves as someone with a disability, or because doing so feels like an admission of something they were raised to overcome. Teaching your son that self-advocacy is a skill, not a concession, and that the accommodations available to him in adult systems are tools not admissions, equips him for a transition that catches many ADHD students off guard.

The endpoint of the self-advocacy work is a young man who does not need anyone to manage his life for him, who has the self-knowledge to design environments that work for his brain, and who has the relational skills to ask for what he needs. That outcome is not guaranteed by any strategy in this book. But it is significantly more likely for a son who has spent years with a parent who believed it was possible and worked toward it consistently.

The Parent You Are Becoming Through This Process

There is something that happens to parents who have been raising a child with ADHD for years that does not get acknowledged often enough. The patience that you did not know you had. The creativity you developed because standard approaches did not work and you had to find other ones. The capacity to hold complexity without collapsing it into a simple explanation. The specific kind of empathy that comes from watching someone you love struggle with something you cannot fix, from learning to sit with difficulty instead of solving it away.

These are not small things. They are qualities that most people spend decades trying to develop and that this particular parenting experience tends to build, not always gracefully, not always on the timeline you would have chosen, but reliably and genuinely. The parent who has navigated five years of ADHD parenting is not the same person who started. She has been changed by it, in ways that are more lasting than any strategy she learned along the way.

This is not a call to reframe the difficulty as a gift, because the difficulty is real and has a real cost. It is an observation about what also happens alongside the difficulty, to the person who stays present and engaged with a genuinely hard thing over time. The quality of attention you bring to your son, the willingness to repair rather than defend, the capacity to see the person behind the behavior, the refusal to give up on a child who makes it difficult not to: these are not natural gifts distributed randomly. They are capacities you have built.

The endpoint that this book has been working toward is not a child who no longer struggles. It is a child who knows how to struggle effectively. And alongside that: a parent who knows how to support someone who is struggling, without losing herself in it, without needing it to be resolved in order to be okay, and without confusing her love for the child with the certainty that the child will be fine. The uncertainty about how his story ends is permanent. The quality of the relationship you are building with him across the years is not uncertain at all.

You are doing something hard. You are doing it with more skill than you started with, more knowledge than you had before, and more capacity for the specific demands of this particular child than any parent who has not done this work could bring. That is not nothing. It is, in fact, most of what he needs.

One final thing deserves to be said, because it is true and it is almost never said: raising a child with ADHD also has a specific texture of joy that parents who have not done it do not experience in the same way. The hyperfocus that locks your son into a project for three hours and produces something remarkable. The laugh at the completely unexpected angle he takes on a situation because his thinking does not travel the conventional path. The moment when the skills you have been building quietly across months of hard work are suddenly visible in an interaction you did not engineer. The particular quality of closeness that develops between a parent and a child when they have been through genuinely difficult things together and have come through without the relationship breaking.

None of this cancels the hard parts. The hard parts are hard. But the complete picture of what this parenting experience is includes both, and the parent who has been doing this long enough knows that the complete picture is more interesting, more human, and ultimately more valuable than either the difficult version or the optimistic version alone. You are living something real. That is worth something.

Conclusion

You made it to the end of this book. That matters, not as an achievement, but as evidence. A parent who reads to the end of a book about raising a son with ADHD is a parent who is still in it, still looking for ways to understand better, still refusing to settle for the most available explanation. That refusal is one of the most important things you can offer your son.

This book did not promise you a solution, and it did not deliver one. What it tried to do was give you a more accurate picture: of what ADHD is and is not, of what strategies have evidence behind them and which ones are folklore, of what the systems around your son can do and what they cannot, and of what your own role in this is and is not. Accuracy is not a comfort. But it is more useful than comfort, and more lasting.

There are a few things worth saying now that you are at the end, before you close this and return to the actual work of parenting.

Progress in ADHD parenting does not look the way progress is supposed to look. It does not accumulate visibly. It does not produce weekly improvements that you can chart and confirm. It arrives in moments you did not plan for, in a transition that was calmer than last time, in a conversation that went differently than the last hundred identical ones, in the way your son walked into a room and handled something that six months ago would have ended badly. You may not notice it when it happens. You will notice it when you look back from a few years further along, and the gap between then and now will be larger than you expected.

In the meantime, on the days when the gap is not visible, the most useful thing you can do is not start over from the beginning. It is to return to the first thing that actually worked for your particular son, in your particular family, in your particular circumstances. Not the first chapter of this book. The first strategy, the first approach, the first moment of connection or structure or understanding that produced something real. That is the thread. Pull it.

The relationship you have with your son is the most important thing in this entire book. More important than any strategy, any system, any accommodation, any medication. The strategies work better inside a strong relationship. The systems hold better when the child feels known by the adult implementing them. The repair is possible because the relationship is worth repairing. And the repair is what he will remember, far more than the rupture that made it necessary.

Your son does not need you to be a perfect parent. He needs you to be a present one. Present enough, often enough, with enough self-knowledge to recognize when you are not and enough willingness to come back when you have been away. That is achievable. On most days, in most moments, it is already what you are doing.

What this book has tried to give you is not a set of instructions to execute. It is a framework for thinking about a child who does not fit standard frameworks, and a set of tools for the specific situations that come with raising him. Some of those tools will fit your son and your family and this particular season of his development. Others will not. Your job is not to implement everything. It is to know enough that you can recognize which tool belongs in which situation and to have enough confidence in your own judgment that you can use it.

The child you are raising is going to grow into a person you cannot yet fully predict. That is true of all children, but it is more true of ADHD children, whose trajectories are less constrained by conventional expectations and whose outcomes are less predictable from current performance than their neurotypical peers. The version of your son who exists ten years from now is not the sum of today's difficulties. He is the sum of every investment you have made in his sense of himself, his capacity to manage his own brain, and his knowledge that at least one person in his life has always believed that the best version of him is real and achievable.

That person is you. Go back to what worked. Stay in the relationship. The rest follows.

References

Barkley, R. A. (2012). Executive functions: What they are, how they work, and why they evolved. Guilford Press.

Barkley, R. A. (2013). Taking charge of ADHD: The complete, authoritative guide for parents (3rd ed.). Guilford Press.

Barkley, R. A. (2015). Attention-deficit hyperactivity disorder: A handbook for diagnosis and treatment (4th ed.). Guilford Press.

Brooks, R., & Goldstein, S. (2001). Raising resilient children: Fostering strength, hope, and optimism in your child. McGraw-Hill.

Brown, B. (2010). The gifts of imperfection: Let go of who you think you're supposed to be and embrace who you are. Hazelden.

Brown, T. E. (2013). A new understanding of ADHD in children and adults: Executive function impairments. Routledge.

Cooper-Kahn, J., & Dietzel, L. (2008). Late, lost, and unprepared: A parents' guide to helping children with executive functioning. Woodbine House.

Dawson, P., & Guare, R. (2010). Executive skills in children and adolescents: A practical guide to assessment and intervention (2nd ed.). Guilford Press.

Deater-Deckard, K. (2004). Parenting stress. Yale University Press.

Diamond, A. (2013). Executive functions. Annual Review of Psychology, 64, 135–168.

Faraone, S. V., Asherson, P., Banaschewski, T., Biederman, J., Buitelaar, J. K., Ramos-Quiroga, J. A., Rohde, L. A., Sonuga-Barke, E. J. S., Tannock, R., & Franke, B. (2015). Attention-deficit/hyperactivity disorder. Nature Reviews Disease Primers, 1, 15020.

Gathercole, S. E., & Alloway, T. P. (2008). Working memory and learning: A practical guide for teachers. SAGE.

Gross, J. J. (Ed.). (2014). Handbook of emotion regulation (2nd ed.). Guilford Press.

Hallowell, E. M., & Ratey, J. J. (2011). Driven to distraction: Recognizing and coping with attention deficit disorder (rev. ed.). Anchor Books.

Hoza, B., Martin, C. P., Pirog, A., & Shoulberg, E. K. (2016). Using physical activity to manage ADHD symptoms: The state of the evidence. Current Psychiatry Reports, 18(12), 113.

Johnston, C., & Mash, E. J. (2001). Families of children with attention-deficit/hyperactivity disorder: Review and recommendations for future research. Clinical Child and Family Psychology Review, 4(3), 183–207.

Kazdin, A. E. (2008). The Kazdin method for parenting the defiant child. Houghton Mifflin.

Maslach, C., & Leiter, M. P. (2016). Understanding the burnout experience: Recent research and its implications for psychiatry. World Psychiatry, 15(2), 103–111.

Mikami, A. Y. (2010). The importance of friendship for youth with attention-deficit/hyperactivity disorder. Clinical Child and Family Psychology Review, 13(2), 181–198.

Neff, K. D. (2011). Self-compassion: The proven power of being kind to yourself. William Morrow.

Nigg, J. T. (2006). What causes ADHD? Understanding what goes wrong and why. Guilford Press.

Pelsser, L. M., Frankena, K., Toorman, J., Savelkoul, H. F., Dubois, A. E., Pereira, R. R., Haagen, T. A., Rommelse, N. N., & Buitelaar, J. K. (2011). Effects of a restricted elimination diet on the behaviour of children with attention-deficit hyperactivity disorder (INCA study): A randomised controlled trial. The Lancet, 377(9764), 494–503.

Pliszka, S. R. (2007). Pharmacologic treatment of attention-deficit/hyperactivity disorder: Efficacy, safety and mechanisms of action. Neuropsychology Review, 17(1), 61–72.

Ratey, J. J., & Hagerman, E. (2008). Spark: The revolutionary new science of exercise and the brain. Little, Brown.

Shaywitz, S. E. (2003). Overcoming dyslexia: A new and complete science-based program for reading problems at any level. Knopf.

Sibley, M. H. (2016). Parent-teen therapy for executive function deficits and ADHD: Building skills and motivation. Guilford Press.

Siegel, D. J., & Bryson, T. P. (2011). The whole-brain child: 12 revolutionary strategies to nurture your child's developing mind. Delacorte.

Sonuga-Barke, E. J. S., Brandeis, D., Cortese, S., Daley, D., Ferrin, M., Holtmann, M., Stevenson, J., Danckaerts, M., van der Oord, S., Dopfner, M., Dittmann, R. W., Simonoff, E., Zuddas, A., Banaschewski, T., Buitelaar, J., Coghill, D., Sergeant, J., Steinhausen, H. C., Stringaris, A., & Taylor, E. (2013). Nonpharmacological interventions for ADHD: Systematic review and meta-analyses of randomized controlled trials of dietary and psychological treatments. American Journal of Psychiatry, 170(3), 275–289.

Steinberg, L. (2014). Age of opportunity: Lessons from the new science of adolescence. Houghton Mifflin Harcourt.

Wolraich, M. L., Hagan, J. F., Allan, C., Chan, E., Davison, D., Earls, M., Evans, S. W., Flinn, S. K., Froehlich, T., Frost, J., Holbrook, J. R., Lehmann, C. U., Lessin, H. R., Okechukwu, K., Pierce, K. L., Winner, J. D., & Zurhellen, W. (2019). Clinical practice guideline for the diagnosis, evaluation, and treatment of attention-deficit/hyperactivity disorder in children and adolescents. Pediatrics, 144(4), e20192528.

www.ingramcontent.com/pod-product-compliance
Lightning Source LLC
LaVergne TN
LVHW052325200926
848481LV00002B/667